River
Cruising Guide

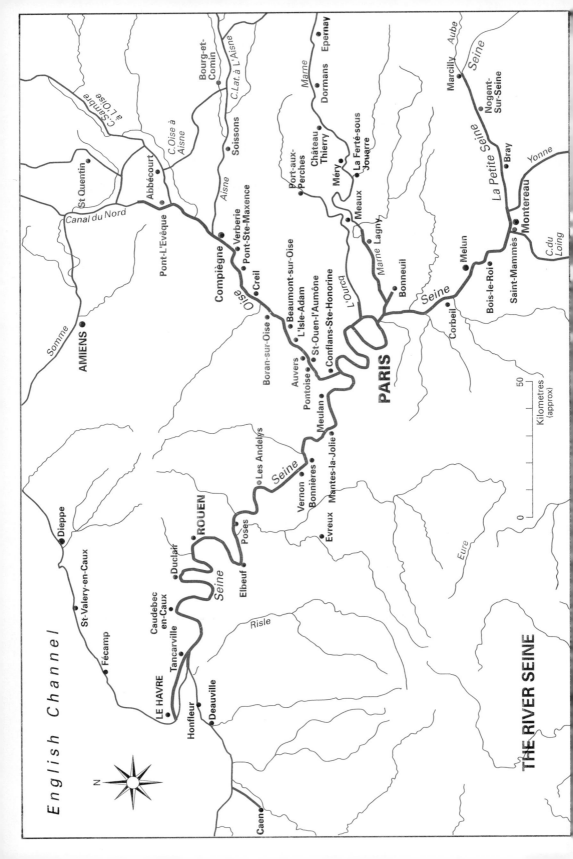

River Seine
Cruising Guide

DEREK BOWSKILL

Imray Laurie Norie & Wilson Ltd
St Ives Cambridgeshire England

Published by
Imray Laurie Norie & Wilson Ltd
Wych House, St Ives, Huntingdon,
Cambridgeshire, PE17 4BT, England
☎ +44 (0)1480 462114 *Fax* +44 (0)1480 496109

ISBN 0 85288 289 0

British Library Cataloguing in Publication Data.
A catalogue record for this book is available from the British Library.

British Library Cataloguing in Publication Data
A catalogue record for this title is available from the British Library.

CAUTION
Every effort has been made to ensure the accuracy of this book. It
contains selected information and thus is not definitive and does not
include all known information on the subject in hand; this is particularly relevant to the plans, which should not be used for navigation.
The author and publishers believe that its selection is a useful aid to
prudent navigation, but the safety of a vessel depends ultimately on
the judgement of the navigator, who should assess all information,
published or unpublished.

CORRECTIONS
The author would be glad to receive any corrections, information or
suggestions which readers may consider would improve the book, as
new impressions will be required from time to time. Letters should
be addressed to the publishers. The more precise the information the
better, but even partial or doubtful information is helpful, if it is
made clear what the doubts are.

The last input of technical information was July 1996.

Printed in Great Britain by
Imray Laurie Norie & Wilson Ltd

Contents

Preface

The river Seine is not the longest, the biggest, the widest, the fastest nor the busiest of continental Europe's waterways; but it must have more appeal and joy per kilometre for cruising Brits than almost any other. Up and down, up and down I have wandered and never ceased to enjoy the contrasts: isolated bankside moorings; a mighty (and sometimes mighty sinister) seaway and estuary; heavy working ports and industrial complexes; marinas, many and various, housing craft from the minuscule to the magnificent and majestic; hamlets, villages and small towns clustered on the banks – with little apparently changed over decades ... and all delighted to welcome waterborne visitors; the river traffic, from oil drum punts and single floating fishermen to the still splendid though dwindling fleets of *péniches*; the massive downstream locks and the miniature machines near the head of navigation; and, commanding the river from its pride of place above (in every way) Rouen and Le Havre, the superb capital, Paris.

I hope I have managed to capture the unique attraction of this magnificent river and the first-rate cruising grounds it provides.

Derek Bowskill
Valcon 1996

Acknowledgements

I would like to thank the officers of the VNF (Voies Navigable de France) at national and local level for their friendly and informed help. This applies also to the lock-keepers – most of whom have made 'new resolutions' and are, on the whole, pretty kind and considerate to those of us *plaisanciers* who don't always understand ... and don't always get it right.

I would also like to thank the many shop-keepers, market vendors, bar-keepers and restaurateurs (all splendid patrons, indeed) who have made the research for this guide such an enjoyable experience.

Dedication

This book is offered in memoriam.

For Wendy Williams: foolishly lost and now beyond recall.

Nearly five decades have passed since we planned to go to France. We never made that journey, *mea culpa*, and I have recently learned of her untimely death in Australia.

Getting there

Crossings

Charts
Imray *C12, C31, C32*
Admiralty *2675, 2450, 2656, 2146, 1349, 2990, 2994, 2880*

Pilot books
The Shell Channel Pilot, Tom Cunliffe, Imray
Macmillan Almanac

This is a guide to the river Seine from estuary to head of navigation; from Le Havre to Marcilly. Since it is not a sea guide, there is no place for detailed passage or pilot-age notes of Channel crossings, but there are lots of cruising folk for whom a long straight Channel crossing to Le Havre is a consummation devoutly not to be wished. So it is worth noting that there are more ways than one of getting to the cruisable stretches of the Seine. In brief, there are three schemes:

1. Directly to Le Havre or Honfleur, or one of the nearby small ports of Fécamp, St-Valéry en Caux, Trouville/Deauville or Ouistreham – intending to go straight up the Seine to Rouen on the next leg;
2. To Le Havre via one or more of the harbours to the east or west: Cherbourg, Dieppe, Le Tréport, Le Touquet or Boulogne – intending to move on through (or into) Le Havre as and when convenient;
3. To Calais – intending to move down through the canals of Picardie and the Pas de Calais to Paris or Conflans Ste Honorine ... avoiding a long Channel crossing, the Seine estuary and its tidal stretch to Amfreville.

Scheme No. 1

For those who do not mind longish crossings, the attractions are twofold: a trip accomplished in one unbroken stint, followed by a comfortable berth in an appealing haven, lingering until time and tide are right for an easy ride up the Seine. (The excep-tion to the havenly aspect is Le Havre itself; while it has a lot going for it as a port of entry, a marina and (with Harfleur) a resort of some appeal, most of it is at a great distance from the marinas.)

LE HAVRE

The harbour can be entered at all times and states – but with weather it gets extreme-ly short, sharp and rough. The buoyed channel has 15m and the marina has 3m.
Marks Fuel tanks, high buildings, 2 red & white chimneys, with the big church tower and white signal tower near.
Visitors Once inside the breakwaters, the marina is immediately to port, and visitors' berths are the first.

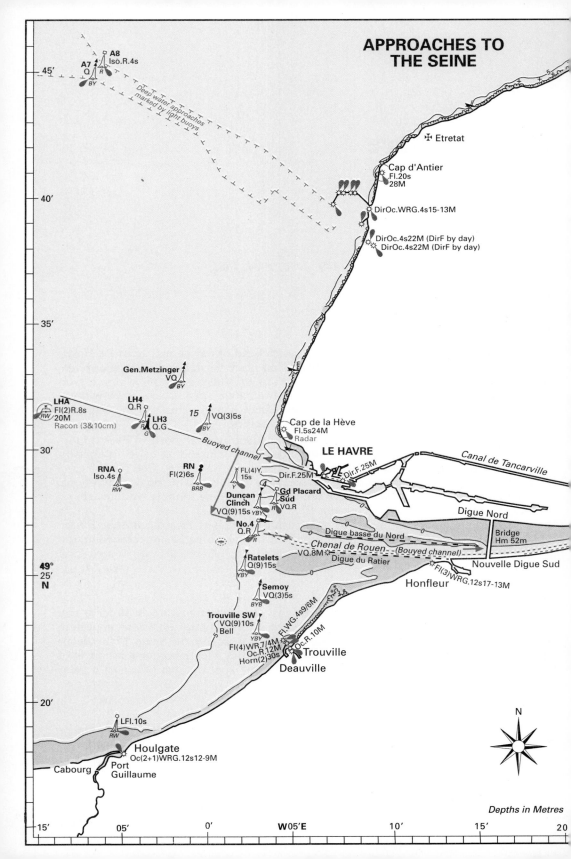

APPROACHES TO THE SEINE

A8 Iso.R.4s

A7 Q BY

Deep water approaches marked by light buoys

⌖ Etretat

Cap d'Antier
Fl.20s
28M

DirOc.WRG.4s15-13M

DirOc.4s22M (DirF by day)
DirOc.4s22M (DirF by day)

Gen.Metzinger VQ BY

LHA Fl(2)R.8s 20M
Racon (3&10cm)
RW

LH4 Q.R

LH3 Q.G R G

15 VQ(3)5s BY

Buoyed channel

Cap de la Hève
Fl.5s24M
Radar

LE HAVRE

Canal de Tancarville

RNA Iso.4s RW

RN Fl(2)6s BRB

Fl(4)Y 15s Y

Dir.F.25M Dir.F.25M

Digue Nord

Duncan Clinch
VQ(9)15s YBY

Gd Placard Sud R VQ.R

Bridge Hm 52m

No.4 Q.R R

Digue basse du Nord

Chenal de Rouen - (Bouyed channel)

VQ.8M

Digue du Ratier

Nouvelle Digue Sud

Ratelets Q(9)15s YBY

Fl(3)WRG.12s17-13M

Honfleur

Semoy VQ(3)5s BYB

Trouville SW
VQ(9)10s
Bell
YBY

Fl.WG.4s9/6M

Oc.R.10M

Fl(4)WR.7/4M
Oc.R.12M
Horn(2)30s

Trouville

Deauville

LFl.10s
RW

Houlgate
Oc(2+1)WRG.12s12-9M

Cabourg

Port Guillaume

N

Depths in Metres

45'

40'

35'

30'

49°
25'
N

20'

15'

15'   05'   0'   **W05'E**   10'   15'   20

HONFLEUR

Until recently it was not possible to combine a visit with a passage up river, but the whole harbour is now locked and consequently more accessible than before. Leisure craft use the inner basin, entry into which is governed by the opening of the bridge across what used to be a locked basin. To gain the best tide and time to go upstream for Rouen means steaming past Honfleur at or shortly after LW. Honfleur's bridge opens three or four times a day: each opening is on the hour after the first opening, which is governed by the time of the Seine tides. (If you have it in mind to use Honfleur, the best plan is to contact the Cercle Nautique de Honfleur for current tidal and bridge information. Write or phone them at CNH, Club House, 8 rue Saint Antoine, BP 118, 14600 Honfleur. ☎ 02 31 98 87 13. They also publish a most helpful brochure.)

FECAMP

This small essentially yachting harbour can usually be entered at better than half tide.
Marks The black-roofed church, a cliff-top signal station, and a collection of towers and spires.
Visitors Pontoons to starboard, or lock into the Bassin Bérigny, straight ahead, which works from approximately 2 hours before until HW.

ST VALERY EN CAUX

A small harbour taking many yachts. The outer harbour dries, with entry no better than half tide. The lock opens 2 hours either side of HW and the road bridge on the hour and the half; there are waiting buoys.
Marks Radio mast and large white building to the east; breakwaters and white lighthouse.
Visitors The lock-keeper will direct you.

FECAMP

The name may have come from the Norse *fiske*, for fish, but it may also have come from the Latin *fict campus*, for the legendary fig field (see below). Once this tiny town was not only a big religious centre, but also the capital of Normandy. Its influence on matters of state declined only when the Norman Dukes began to look seaward and to pay more attention to England. The ruins of the ducal palace can be seen opposite the church of the Holy Trinity.

The small harbour was France's most important cod base, hosting all the boats from the fishing grounds of the Newfoundland Banks, and very active until the late 1980s. That has mainly given way to coastal fishing and EU imports, and Fécamp is now a resort, more devoted to its links with the Benedictines, their famous liqueur and the even more famous consumer of it, Guy de Maupassant. Known as the 'Gate of Heaven', its monastery dates from the 7th century, when it was devoted to another inestimable liquid, the Precious Blood. This relic came, allegedly, with the fig tree in which Joseph of Arimathea (or possibly Nicodemus) had hidden a phial of Christ's blood. This was supposedly washed up on the shores of Fécamp, where a spring of water immediately gushed. This is the spring that feeds the fountain of the Precious Blood. The phial of Holy Blood became one of the relics of Fécamp abbey, which was once the principal pilgrimage in Normandy, with dukes and grandees coming for Easter with their entourages and spreading the word. Less aristocratic visitors still throng to the relic on the Tuesday and Thursday after Trinity.

As if not satisfied with one miraculous claim to posterity and heavenly glory, the Holy Trinity church, built by Richard II, was struck by lightning and burned, but (something in common with the Phoenix) further life was derived from the incineration in the form of the famous Angel's Footprint. Situated to the right of the altar, it is said to derive from a visitation in 943 by an angel pilgrim who issued certain commands and then disappeared in a flash of light, leaving the footprint in the stone. It is not as big as the Buddha's in Sri Lanka, but it has its admirers nevertheless.

As indeed has the Benedictine Palace museum, where in 1510 the monk Bernardo Vincelli first distilled the brew of local plants and spices which later became Benedictine, to be marketed in 1863 by the entrepreneur Alexander Le Grand. On discovering the secret, he did a good deal and made a great deal more. In the museum, you can see a well-documented history of the liqueur, with the 27 growing ingredients, the copper stills and the oak vats that all play a part in the creation of the famous elixir – the tasting of which must make a stopover here a real temptation.

The Newfoundland and Fishing Museum is also an attraction. The first floor shows herring: drift netting, various boats and fishing methods as well as salting and navigation gear.

TROUVILLE AND DEAUVILLE

These two are not only popular yacht harbours, but host fishing fleets. Thus, in general, traffic and the shortage of berths are the main hazards. The entrance dries, but once inside there is 3m in Trouville and better than 2m in Deauville.

Marks Tall, pale Trouville casino; breakwater; apartment blocks.

Visitors Starboard for the marina or straight ahead for the Trouville basin. There is a choice of the Deauville marina or the Trouville basin. Both of these are locked: Deauville works 3 hours either side of HW and Trouville from 1½ before to 2 hours after.

DEAUVILLE

Deauville, in spite of its Channel climate, which can never rival that of France's Mediterranean coast, is an international byword for coastal luxury: a veritable seaside dolce vita. It offers a plethora of entertainment, the much-flaunted sea-water swimming pool being a basic and permanent ingredient, with regular infusions of fîtes, galas, rallies, regattas, car rallies and perhaps above all racing. The season in Deauville, one of the busiest in France, opens in July and ends with the Grand Prix in August. The horses go flat at La Touques and flat and steeple at Clairefontaine. The Planches (a planked but superior beach promenade), the Pompeiian Baths, the Soleil Bar and the Boulevard Eugene-Cornuche all speak of the elegance for which Deauville is renowned. However, in spite of the regular descents by the rich and famous, it has managed to retain most of its old and singular charm.

OUISTREHAM

Ouistreham, at the mouth of the Caen canal and Orne river, is busy with fishing, coasters and ferries, so yachts must be patient. The entry is always better than 2m and the canal is dredged to 9m.

Marks Red-topped white lighthouse by the lock.

Visitors Waiting pontoon to port; there are two locks that work from 2 hours before to 3 hours after HW. After locking, the marina is to port.

Scheme No. 2

For those who want no more than a staging post and a break before moving directly up the Seine to Rouen.

CHERBOURG

The well-known, well-used port is given over to commerce, ferries and the navy. It can be entered at any time and state.

Marks High flats, churches and many other buildings are prominent; huge harbour walls and forts; water towers.
Visitors The marina, to the west of the Gare Maritime, is towards the centre after entering through the east or west Passe.

DIEPPE

Dieppe is a ferry terminal and fishing port and can be entered at any time and state. It is dredged to better than 3m. Traffic is the main hazard.
Marks Chalk cliffs; a tall church spire and signal stations to the east; the castle is to the west.
Visitors The locked Basin Duquesne, tending to starboard and then straight ahead; the lock works from 2 hours before to 1 hour after HW. There is also a lifting bridge. There is a waiting pontoon nearby.

BOULOGNE

Since this is France's most important fishing port and extremely busy with ferry and commercial shipping, its traffic must be negotiated with care; otherwise the approach is without hazard. On the plus side, the harbour can be entered at all times and states.
Marks Cathedral cupola, harbour breakwaters and tall pillar east of the entrance.
Visitors The marina or the Quai Gambetta.

Scheme No. 3

For those who dislike hours at sea, and want to explore only the calmer aspects of the Seine – and to do so with the added appeal of some more of the French inland waterways.

CALAIS

The nearest French port to England. While there are shallows and sandbanks in the offing, the real hazard is the heavy and speedy commercial traffic. The harbour can be entered at all times and states, but with weather it gets extremely short, sharp and rough, and is to be avoided. The buoyed channel has 8m and the marina something less.
Marks The white lighthouse is obvious, and ferries will show the way.
Visitors Waiting buoys near the lock; yacht basin bridge opens (usually 3 times) between 1h hours before and h hour after HW. Just before opening an orange light is shown, then green for entering, red for leaving

Channel crossings

The most popular ports for quitting the UK and crossing the Channel definitely come in clusters, twinned with their destinations on the other side. First come the easterly ports of Ramsgate, Dover, Folkestone, and Rye. Their traditional ports of call are Calais, Dunkerque and Boulogne, with the experimental taking a chance with Le Touquet and St-Valéry sur Somme.

Next are the central ports, comprising the quartet of Newhaven, Brighton, Shoreham and Littlehampton, the conglomerate of all the Solent harbours from Selsey Bill to the Needles, and, slightly out on a limb, Poole and Weymouth. Their usual targets lie between Dieppe and Cherbourg, Le Havre being perhaps the most used, with the smaller harbours and havens of the Baie de la Seine being left for those with an affinity for the esoteric.

Finally, there are the more westerly points of departure. They are the ports associated with the great spread of Lyme Bay: Torquay, Paignton and Brixham in the cosmopolitan cluster of the eponymous Bay, and the famous two outsiders on each side of Start Point, Dartmouth and Salcombe.

Here are some of the main distances (rounded off to 5 nautical miles) followed by some typical trips:

Ramsgate to Dunkerque 35M
Dover to Calais 20M
Folkestone to Boulogne 25M
Rye to Le Touquet 40M
Newhaven to Dieppe 60M
Brighton to Fécamp 65M
Nab Tower to Fécamp 75M
Nab Tower to Le Havre 85M
Nab Tower to Cherbourg 70M

RAMSGATE TO CALAIS

At no more than 30 nautical miles, this is one of the most popular cross-Channel hops. There are two routes across: to the north and to the south of the Goodwins (three, if you include risking the Goodwins themselves at the top of the tide, as some have hazardously done). The Goodwins are the first but not the only major hazard in the area; the second is the build-up of commercial shipping, from the small fishing vessels off North Foreland, through cross-Channel ferries and hovercraft, to the supertankers that take up to ten miles to stop and two to answer to the helm. Some of these supertankers are so deep-draughted that, in this particular area even in the channels, they steam extremely close to the bottom, thus being severely restricted in their manoeuvres. A southerly passage round the Goodwins is therefore preferable because it naturally offers a 90-degree crossing of the Traffic Separation Zone.

The following extracts from Rule 10 of the *International Regulations for Prevention of Collisions at Sea* are of singular importance in the area:

    c. A vessel shall so far as practicable avoid crossing traffic lanes, but if obliged to do so shall cross as nearly as practicable at right angles to the general direction of the traffic flow.

    j. A vessel of less than 20m or a sailing vessel shall not impede the safe passage of a power-driven vessel following a traffic lane.

The trip is short and straightforward, quitting Ramsgate southward past Brake and through The Downs, to the southerly tip of the Goodwins, roughly one third of the way; then southeasterly across the shipping lanes to the buoyed entrance to Calais. The approach to Calais is usually located by close observation of ferry movements. The offshore hazards are the sandbanks known as the Ridens de Calais and the Ridens de la Rade, and their associated wrecks; however, the approach channel (to the south and west of the Ridens) is well buoyed and lit. Shoresides, there are two conspicuous belfries and a tall lighthouse.

With the distance involved between Ramsgate and Calais, at a speed through the water ranging from 10 to 20 knots, the tidal set will not be of a substantial nature, and normal navigational procedures will be enough to see you across both ways. If anything, however, when going to Calais it is best to favour the westerly stream; the reverse is true when returning. The main precaution is the usual one: noting the forecasts over the previous 48 hours.

BRIGHTON TO FECAMP

Brighton to Fécamp is just over twice the distance of the Ramsgate–Calais trip, but it is nonetheless almost as popular. There is no problem in quitting the marina at Brighton at whatever time you wish, and the trip across is hazard-free, except for the proliferation of traffic.

The distance between Brighton and Fécamp is 65 nautical miles, so at a speed through the water of 10 to 20 knots the trip will take somewhere between three and seven hours. It will be worth noting the tidal set, unless you just happen to have an equally split six hours of three hours east and three hours west. If anything, it is best to favour the easterly stream when bound for France, and the reverse upon the return.

THE SOLENT TO LE HAVRE

With points of departure varying from The Needles to Selsey Bill (including the distant Port Solent), actual distances will be somewhere between 85 and 110M. At these distances, at speeds between 10 and 20 knots you must expect to occupy between four and 12 hours, so proper consideration must be given to tidal set. Favour the easterly stream when on passage to France and the westerly when returning.

The factors affecting your departure time will be mainly concerned with weather and domestics. Many people favour a night crossing with a dawn sighting of the French coast, and there is a lot to be said for that unless it is a rushed Friday job after a fraught week at the office. The most important precaution is to listen to weather and shipping forecasts well in advance so that you can form a proper perception of what is going on and therefore likely to happen: merely the latest forecast is not really good enough.

POOLE TO CHERBOURG

At just over 60 nautical miles, with the well known EC1 buoy designating the halfway mark on a basically southerly course, this is as popular as the Brighton–Fécamp trip. Since the passage time will be between three and six hours, here again it will be worth noting the tidal set, unless you are at the top of the tide with equal three hours east and three hours west. From here, as well, it is best to favour the easterly stream when on passage for Cherbourg and the westerly when returning to Poole. There is no locking problem when leaving Poole harbour, and the restraints will be the two mentioned above: domestic and weather. Once across, the approach to Cherbourg is hazard-free.

The River Seine from sea to source

Seine Maritime – the sea to Rouen

The older version of the river Seine's name was 'Seqouine' coming from the Latin *sequana*, or from the Celtic *squan*, meaning to curve or bend – the river being likened to a giant serpent. But from where or whatever, we still have a 'Winding River', and by the simple expedient of losing a letter or two the name of the river reduced itself to its present form: the Seine.

It starts (or rises) near Oigny, not far from Dijon in Burgundy, and stops (or falls) into the Channel (La Manche) at Le Havre. In all it flows for 782km. It is navigable for the 517km from Le Havre to Marcilly, where it joins the river Aube and the now disused Haute-Seine canal. The 67m difference in water levels between Marcilly and the sea is managed by 25 locks.

After its earlier more illustrious, classical appellations, the present river seems no longer satisfied with its contemporary version as Seine pure and simple, and has had created for it a number of variations: from Le Havre to Rouen it is the Seine-Maritime; from Rouen to Paris, the Basse-Seine; from Paris to the Yonne, the Haute-Seine; and from the Yonne to Marcilly, the Petite-Seine. And indeed, streaming and descending, it is a river of such magnitude and magnificence that it deserves its distinctions and niceties. Sweeping successively through Champagne, Ile de France and Normandy, the valley of the Seine displays not only its natural beauty, but also its grandeur and its history in all its castles, fortresses and a multitude of other riverside edifices.

As with most rivers, the banks on the outside bends of the river are the ones that take the thrust, while the inner ones, deserted by speedy progress and left to their own more leisurely inclinations, become slowly but inexorably and progressively silted. On the Seine this process has had its way for centuries, and the silting and undercutting banks have considerably altered the river's course, especially in its downstream reaches. The relentless erosion has created ever-growing depressions and indentations, so that some of the inner bends have extended into vast arcs of sediment, developing every decade.

The other side of the coin (perhaps 'sequoine') is the effect of the force of the current on the outside bends, which, of course, after centuries of scouring, carry the deepest water. Where this occurs at a confluence with an incoming stream the junction makes an obvious choice for a haven. If it were a major tributary that entered it would almost inevitably become a preferred site for a river port. When the deep cutting occurred at a bend with a steep cliff it was, in olden days, clearly ideal for a lookout and fortress. Jewels in these crowned cliffs are such fortresses as Gaillard at Les Andelys and those of Robert the Devil at La Bouille; other well known locations are Caudebec and Rouen, which last has exploited its situation to become the substantial port it is today.

Although there is no long succession of oxbows, there have been many close encounters of that kind. Particularly near the estuary, there are many old-established eminences and promontories that have been, if not literally abolished, then severely reduced to little more than nearly isolated mini-headlands. Examples of this triangular truncation are in evidence at Quillebeuf, La Roque, Cap Le Hode and Tancarville Point.

Le Havre is a large sea port, dating back to the 16th century. It may not be the most charismatic of French ports, but it is efficient, has comprehensive services, is not expensive, and for British boaters is not only the Gateway to the Ocean, as the French call it (Porte Océane), but also Front Door to Paris and the French inland waterways system. Le Havre is a commercially well-used port and town, and while it is not without appeal, most of it is well distanced from the harbour, so that for our purposes it has to be considered merely as a way in. Until recently Le Havre was virtually the only feasible port of entry, but the new lock and general improvements to the system at Honfleur have made a difference, offering skippers a little more flexibility and a most inviting alternative. (Please see Honfleur below.) Do not overlook the fact that the low bridges at Rouen deny access to the marina pontoons to craft with more than 6m air draught.

LE HAVRE

The deep-water port of Le Havre is second only to Marseille in France's ranking and fifth in the EU, coping with more than 8,000 big ships from America, Africa, the East and the UK. It has a long history.

In 1517, a new port was decreed to replace the silted-up Harfleur. The following year the first warship, the *Hermine*, entered, and the king somewhat grudgingly granted the town his name, François de Grace, and his arms. However, it was not until the American War of Independence that trading and long-distance shipping got under way, at first with supplies for The Rebels. Later, the direction of trade reversed when cotton, coffee and tobacco came in.

As time passed, the transatlantic route became more popular and the voyage time became shorter, until in 1850 the *Franklin*, with paddles and sails, crossed in 14 days. In 1864 came the steamship *Washington*, to be followed by such legends in their lifetimes as the *Normandie* and the *Ile de France*.

Unfortunately for skipper and crew, the delights of the town are at a goodly distance from the marinas, but there are some sights that deserve the walk. The specially designed Place de l'Hôtel de Ville is a vast and impressive area; lawns and trees are surrounded by architect-designed buildings, all risen from the wartime devastation, which is remembered in Adam's *Wounded Birds* memorial sculpture. Avenue Foch is another planning achievement: a promenade with more lawns and trees, and more designer buildings, all leading to the first and last sentinel: Ocean Gate.

St Joseph's church, although a somewhat sombre edifice, has the distinction of an octagonal lantern-house some 109m in height, with stained-glass windows catching light from all angles at all times. St Joseph's is in concrete. In contrast is the André Malraux Arts Museum, in glass and metal, which also possesses a lantern. Known as *The Eye*, it looks, Cyclops-style, out to sea. The museum is intriguingly lit through a slatted blind on its glass roof and by specially filtered electric lights. It houses works by the famous Dufy, who was born in the port, and also Monet, Pissarro, Sisley and Renoir.

The cathedral of Notre Dame has an organ from 1637 with the arms of Richelieu, who presented it. The Old Havre museum is in a restored Norman town house in flint and stone. The Graville abbey had in the 6th century a sanctuary for the relics of Ste Honorine, but these later went up river to Conflans to avoid the marauding Vikings.

The marinas in the Anse des Régates and de Joinville are protected by a vast breakwater and jetty, overlooked by the 52m signal tower, directly under which are moored the pilot boats, as well as the classic liners' tugs, known as *abeilles* – bees. The nearby beach, which is a must for windsurfers, is, in season, picked out by its long line of white-painted wooden beach huts; just like Frinton-on-Sea.

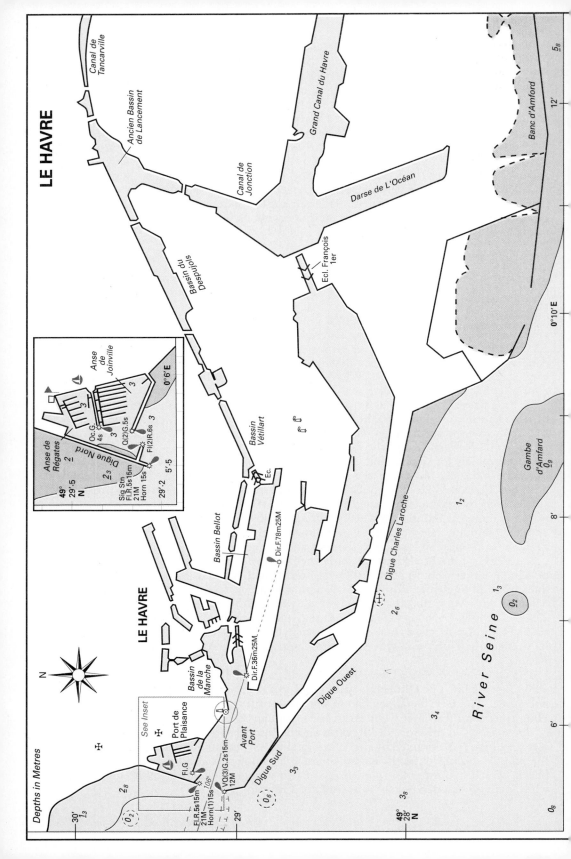

LE HAVRE

Depths in Metres

Canal de Tancarville

Ancien Bassin de Lancement

Grand Canal du Havre

Canal de Jonction

Darse de L'Océan

Banc d'Amford

Bassin du Despujols

Ecl. François 1er

0°10'E

Bassin Vétillart

Ec.

Gambe d'Amford
0_9

Bassin Bellot

Dir.F.78m25M

Digue Charles Laroche

1_2

Dir.F.36m25M

2_6

River Seine 1_3

0_2

Bassin de la Manche

Digue Ouest

3_4

LE HAVRE

N

See Inset

Port de Plaisance

Fl.G

VQ(3)G.2s15m 12M

Avant Port

Digue Sud

3_3

3_8

49°
28'
N

0_8

3_3

0_6

2_8

30'
1_3

0_2

Fl.R.5s15m 21M
Horn(1)15s

116°

29'

49°
28'
N

3_8

INSET:

49° N
29'·5

Anse de Régates
2

2_3

Digue Nord

Anse de Joinville

3
3
3
3
3
3
3

Oc.G. 4s
Q(2)G.5s
Fl(2)R.6s 3

Sig. Stn
Fl.R.5s15m
21M
Horn 15s

29'·2

5'·5

0°6'E

So much for the general, now for the particular: within Le Havre itself, the dockyard complex is a complicated affair. Merchant ships have their own locks, which are known locally as 'SAS' – surely enough of a warning in itself. A *pertuis* is a narrow alley that links basins with the same water level, thus not using a lock. *Pertuis* are usually crossed by a moving bridge. They are, first, the Quinette de Rochemont, leading into the Bellot basin close to the harbour entrance, and second, the FranÁois 1ier, going on further towards Tancarville. Neither is available to leisure craft, which must use the Citadelle basin and negotiate the moving bridge into the Eure basin. Next is Bellot basin, into the Vétillart lock and basin and finally into the Tancarville canal. Citadelle operates on demand 24 hours a day when sea levels permit, although its bridge is closed at certain times. Vétillart lock is open from 0600 to 2230, while Tancarville opens on demand from −4 to +3 HW at Le Havre. Traffic control lights are in operation. Regulations state that life jackets are compulsory for all on board.

Many first-time visitors are tempted to use this inner canal/basin route, believing it to be in every way calmer than the Seine estuary. In my opinion, the superficially appealing and seductive Tancarville Syndrome, which uses the dirty canal water instead of the muddied waters of the estuary for the first leg up the Seine, does not stand up to rigorous challenge. The canal route brings its own challenges: confrontations with low slow bridges, wearisome locks, much commercial traffic and generally unpleasant surroundings. In addition, masts must be lowered in Le Havre before you can pass through the canal. If you use the canal as a last resort to bypass the sea reach, you will probably find that your 'short cut' requires careful organisation and timing with the authorities and may require over 6 hours.

If these options are both perceived as perils, then going for gold with the Seine instead of the dross of Tancarville will seem like avoiding Charybdis only to be attacked by Scylla. However, in my opinion the river is much to be preferred: a less challenging itinerary and, while not actually compelling in its own vistas, nevertheless a more attractive scenic proposition. The first 25km of the river are flanked by training walls, beyond which marshy ground stretches to the hills in the distance. In the 18th century the river covered the full width of this valley, but the training walls were built to contain the spread.

When leaving Le Havre for the Seine, there are various apparent hazards to be avoided. The first is bad weather and the second the big commercial ships that move between Rouen and the sea at an average of 12 a day. They ignore leisure craft.

Nothing can be done about adverse weather conditions, so it is best to stay put and enjoy the shoresides attractions of Le Havre. The big ships, however, are so conspicuous that there is never any problem in seeing them and steering well clear of them. More sinister, inconspicuous dangers lurk in the shoal banks at the entry to the river. Inconspicuous, that is, except for the excellence of the buoyage. The cautious route is westerly to YBY *LH11*, standing off southerly to YBY *Duncan Clinch*, and only then passing the red *No. 4* to access the main channel on an easterly course. After that, you keep just to the north of the channel (as in the Traffic Regulations) and wait for the wide vistas to change to pleasantly wooded cliffs.

Up to Tancarville the Chenal de Rouen is marked by port and starboard buoys lit at night by red and green lights. Above Tancarville there are miniature lighthouses on the banks lit at night mainly by fixed red and green or occasional violet lights. On the inside of each hairpin bend is often a lobe of shallows, usually marked by a buoy apparently in midstream.

The Chenal de Rouen is the dredged channel from the river mouth to off Honfleur. It is kept open only by constant dredging. Some years ago a training wall, the Digue du Ratier, was built to divert the river from its former course along the coast from Honfleur to off Trouville, and the deep channel now runs close parallel to this. The north side of the channel is bounded by shifting mud banks which are shallower than charted and may dry in places. The tidal streams run strongly in this channel (up to

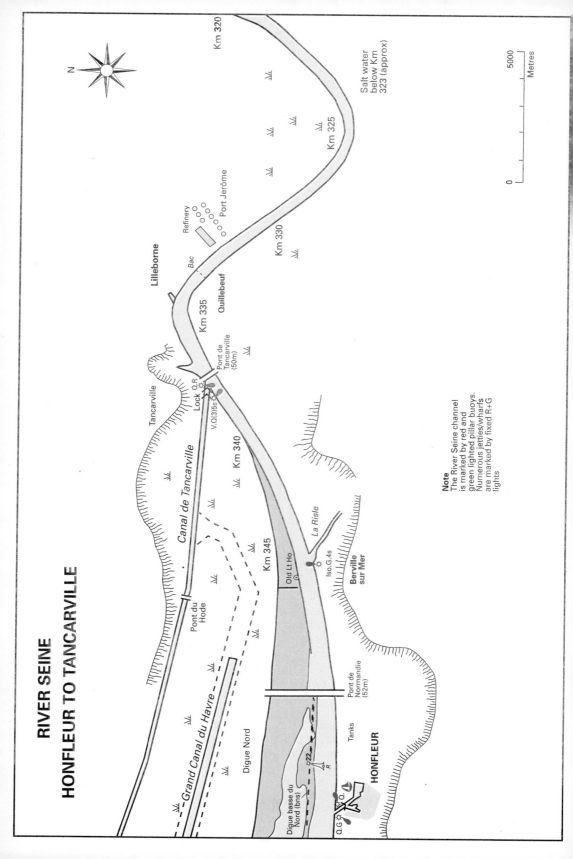

4·5 knots at springs) and with westerly winds over the ebb an unpleasant sea with standing waves is set up. The approaches to the river mouth from both Le Havre and Deauville can be rough in onshore winds because of the shallow water, and on the Le Havre side this is made worse by reflected waves off the Digue Sud.

The river is wide and bleak in its estuary, and it stays that way for a good long stretch after Le Havre and Honfleur; indeed, it must not be overlooked that the estuary is shallow, so that in strong winds between WSW and NW the passage from Deauville or Le Havre to the river mouth can be exceedingly rough. Furthermore, due to the speed of the tide even in calm weather standing waves form in the Chenal de Rouen. Thus, for most of the time it feels like one of the world's major waterways rather than that famous romantic French river dedicated to so many Latin lovers all over the world, and indeed it does seem easier to imagine that L'Inconnue de la Seine took her life in this dead expanse rather than among the fleshpots of the Rive Gauche. In fact, it is not until you begin the final approach to Rouen that the Seine becomes one of those rivers that are perceived as being suitable for cruising down on a Sunday afternoon – and even then it is still a work-horse's outing ... or a water-busman's as it were.

On this mini-odyssey, then, the first place of habitation and note is Honfleur, on the left bank, fascinating enough to be visited in its own right for its own delight. Until recently it was not possible to combine a visit with a passage up river, but the whole harbour is now locked and consequently more accessible than before. Leisure craft use the inner basin, entry into which is governed by the opening of the bridge across what used to be a locked basin. To gain the best tide and time to go upstream for Rouen means steaming past Honfleur at or shortly after LW. Honfleur's bridge opens three or four times a day, on the hour after the first opening.

(If you have it in mind to use Honfleur, the best plan is to contact the Cercle Nautique de Honfleur for current tidal and bridge information. Write or phone them at CNH, Club House, 8 rue Saint Antoine, BP 118, 14600 Honfleur. ☎ 02 31 98 87 13. They also publish a most helpful brochure.)

HONFLEUR

This delightful old town is at the foot of the hill known as the Côte de Grace, its old streets, dock and church blending almost seamlessly. Honfleur was a fortress town up to the late 1400s, and went on to be a famous point of departure for those 17th-century Normans who sought out the western world, and captured, if not captivated, Canada.

Now it is a yachtsman's haven and a painter's dream. The Impressionists gathered here, some preferring the fishing-village ethos to the atmosphere of Big Brother Havre across the way. Many 'names' from a very mixed bag came to stay: Musset, Boudin, Corot, Satie, Sorel. Baudelaire described it as 'the dearest of my dreams', recalling Stevenson's comment about the other coast: 'I was happy at Hyères'. And it is a picturesque place, with the old dock and the governor's house (La Lieutenance), the classic fishing boats and modern yachts creating a pleasing *chiaroscuro*.

The old church of St Stephen is now the Maritime Museum, while the Folk Art Museum is to be found in what used to be the prison. Boudin's memorial square has many old houses, while on Saturdays there is the special attraction of the flower market. His museum in the old chapel is given over in the main to the Honfleur school of estuary painters, but there is a good mix of artefacts from 18th/19th-century Normandy life with pieces by 20th-century painters.

Next on the right bank is the exit to the canal which some readers may feel I have maligned: the Tancarville at PK 338. Also to be seen are some of the first tall radar towers and those vast-span bridges that will later become commonplace.

Above Tancarville the river begins its famous 'sequoine' meanderings, drifting from one side of the valley to the other: one moment under a chalk cliff or a steeply wood-

CANAL DE TANCARVILLE

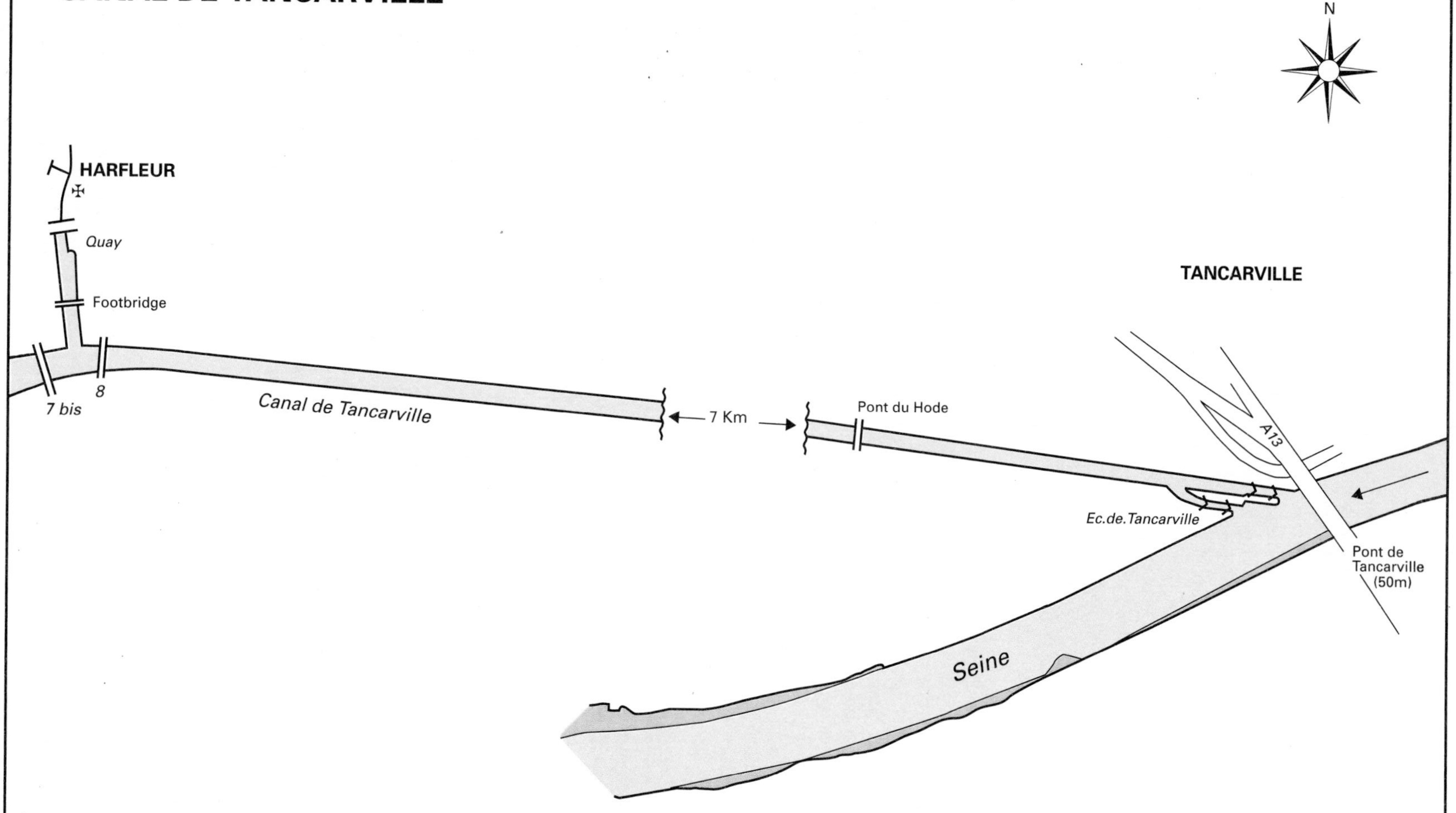

N

HARFLEUR

Quay

Footbridge

7 bis

8

Canal de Tancarville

7 Km

Pont du Hode

TANCARVILLE

A13

Ec.de. Tancarville

Pont de Tancarville (50m)

Seine

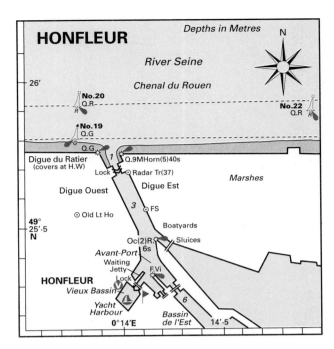

HONFLEUR

Depths in Metres   N

River Seine

Chenal du Rouen

26'

No.20
Q.R
R

No.22
Q.R
R

No.19
Q.G

Q.G
G

Digue du Ratier
(covers at H.W)

1   Q.9MHorn(5)40s

Lock   Radar Tr(37)

Digue Est

Marshes

Digue Ouest

Old Lt Ho

3   FS

49°
25'·5
N

Boatyards

Oc(2)R
6s   Sluices

Avant-Port

Waiting
Jetty

F.Vi

HONFLEUR
Vieux Bassin   Lock

Yacht
Harbour

6

0°14'E

Bassin
de l'Est   14'·5

ed slope, the next coasting gently through flat fields and pastures. The ocean-going ships present a strange picture moving as if through green pastureland, entirely disconnected from the river itself – that is, until you appreciate their deep draught close to, when they not only wash the banks as they pass, but also give that extra 'lift'.

Generally speaking, attempting any kind of break below Rouen is a laborious and perilous affair. In particular, if you are thinking of mooring, there are two main and grave dangers to be considered before even thinking of using the jetties or piles on the river: the first is just being effortlessly and perhaps unknowingly crushed by a big ship, and the second is drying out to find yourself bottoming on harsh to foul to destructive ground. Unfortunately, when it comes to the apparently simple and obvious alternative of anchoring the situation does not improve, and neither does the holding ground. In fact, the general condition of the river bed, the heavy commercial traffic and the aggressive tides combine to make anchoring not only risky, but almost universally deemed to be unsafe.

However, mooring for short periods is tolerated; in fact, it cannot be avoided when cruising from Rouen to the sea during the out-of-season months, which have shorter daylight hours, because of the ban on night travel by leisure craft. It is important to avoid open straight stretches where big ships pass at high speeds, and also mooring too near the bank, since a heavy wash can push you against it or even lift you on to it. Avoid also the apparent safety of inlets, for the same reason. It is prudent to find a spot near a working ferry, since the big ships slow down when passing, causing much less upheaval. The ferrymen and pilots are usually willing to offer advice, especially those stationed at Caudebec. It is essential to let the navigation authorities know if you have to stop; don't forget that correct navigation lights are compulsory throughout the night.

The river stations at Tancarville (PK 337 on the right bank) and Passage du Trait (PK 299 on the left bank opposite Le Trait) can sometimes offer sound mooring possibilities. Leisure craft must tie up between the piles or to the inner (bank) side of commercial craft.

Most quays are reserved for cargo ships and mooring by pleasure boats is prohibited. In any case, most quays have no ladders, are too high to disembark and do not

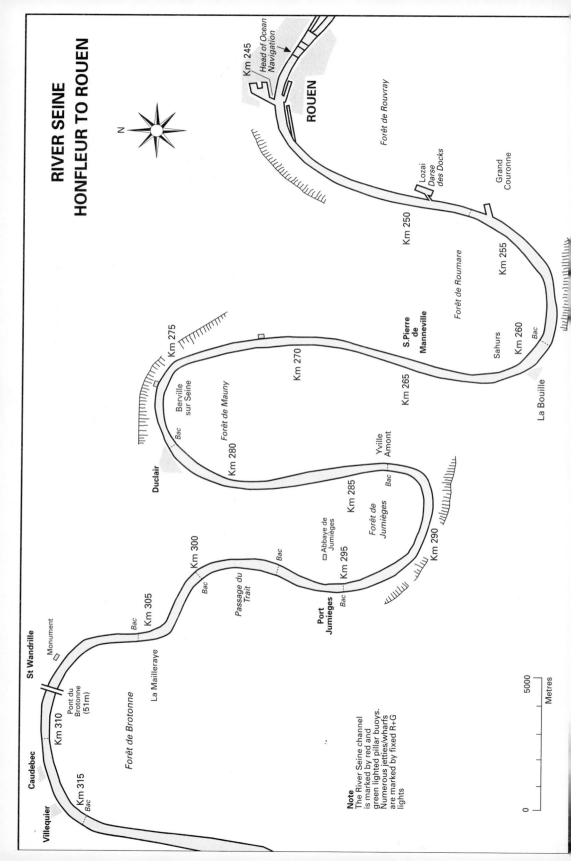

have bollards suitable for small craft. Quays completely forbidden to leisure craft are: Quai de Seine at Honfleur, the Radicatel, Port Jérôme, St-Wandrille, Le Trait, Yainville, and Duclair. However, coming alongside is tolerated at a few places, Quillebeuf and Caudebec being two of the few. Quillebeuf-sur-Seine, a commercial quay at PK 331 on the left bank, is no distance up river, hardly 5km after Tancarville, which we left on the right. Indeed, one after another come the walls and halls of fame as we steam past Quillebeuf-sur-Seine, Villequier at PK 313, Caudebec at PK 310, St-Wandrille at PK 308 and Jumièges at PK 296 – after which it can be a fairly disheartening 50km before the welcoming pontoons at Rouen are reached.

QUILLEBEUF

This small community was originally settled by Viking raiders as a bolt hole and base for baser operations. From such an unblessed but promising beginning it grew into a flourishing port and worked fully until the 1800s. Boats would wait here for the tide, it being an excellent staging post for vessels bound both up and downstream. However, one such, the *Telemaque*, waited too long and sank offshore, reputedly carrying the crown jewels.

Quillebeuf point has a fine tower of a modernist lighthouse, while the church must make do with its unfinished Romanesque tower, although it has a much better 12th-century door and splendid 16th-century chancel and nave.

In between these two, Villequier (PK 313·5) may have a vacant buoy. Leisure craft are allowed to use the buoys only on sufferance. Competent crew must be on board and prepared to cast off at all times. The village is in a beautiful setting and houses the Victor Hugo museum. Strictly speaking, the Villequier buoys are exclusively reserved for merchant ships, and are in non-stop use. There are other buoys on the river that can be used, but there is always some risk, and leisure craft must quit them immediately upon demand, day or night. A 24-hour watch by competent crew is therefore necessary – as well as for the usual traffic/wash safeguards.

VILLEQUIER

Splendidly sited below a high-flying castle poised on wooded hills, this old pilot station was once a thriving spot for the freelances who took craft up or downstream. It is remembered now for the sad event brought about by the *mascaret* (bore). After only 6 months of marriage, Victor Hugo's daughter Léopoldine and her husband Charles were drowned in the river in 1843. The Victor Hugo Museum occupies a house once owned by the husband's boat-building family, and is crowded with memorabilia of Léopoldine collected and created by the grief-stricken Victor Hugo himself. The churchyard contains the tomb of Victor Hugo's wife as well as that of Charles and Léopoldine, who shared a coffin.

CAUDEBEC

Caudebec, not far away at PK 310, is now little more than a commercial quay-place. It must not be forgotten that there is always the danger of drying out on foul ground. Someone should remain on board at all times, not only to adjust lines for the tide, but also to attempt to fend off when the wash of big ships assaults with maximum force. Many are the skippers I have met who have decided or have been 'forced' to tie up on the tidal stretch. All have unpleasant tales to tell.

Caudebec first appears in a monks' charter going back to the 11th century. In the 12th century it was fortified and prepared for attack by English forces – which forces were in the end successful, if wasteful, since they stayed conquerors for only thirty years, the four decades from 1419 to 1449: so much effort for so little gain. After the Religious Troubles, Caudebec surrendered to the religious discipline of Henri IV in 1592. God seems to have been pleased with their Job-like submission, casting a

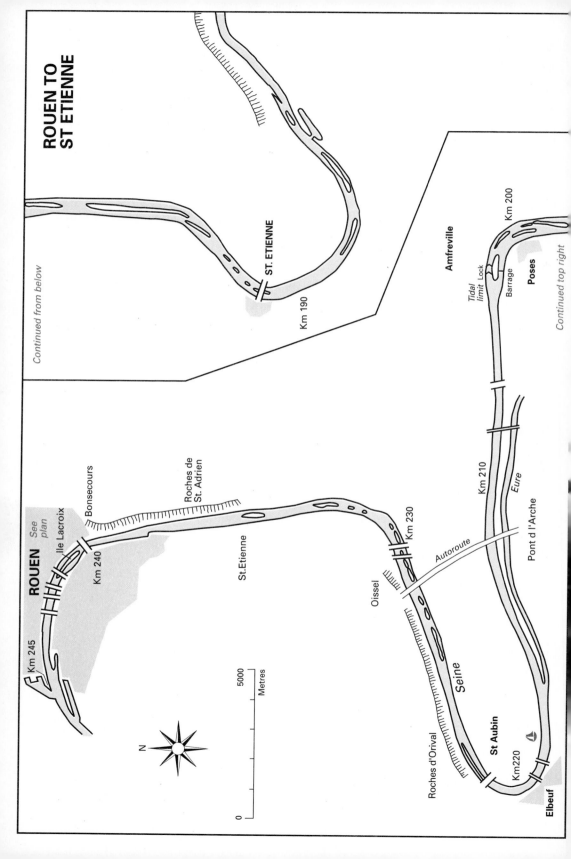

ROUEN TO ST ETIENNE

Continued from below

ST. ETIENNE

Km 190

Continued top right

Amfreville

Tidal limit

Lock

Barrage

Poses

Km 200

Km 210

Eure

Pont d'l'Arche

Autoroute

Bonsecours

Roches de St. Adrien

Ile Lacroix

ROUEN

See plan

Km 240

Km 245

St.Etienne

Oissel

Km 230

Seine

Roches d'Orival

St Aubin

Km220

Elbeuf

N

5000

Metres

0

favourable eye upon their decision and rewarding their virtue with commercial prosperity. Caudebec became a flourishing glove and hat making centre, and at one time was the capital of the Caux region.

The town itself is unusual in layout, having been built in the form of an amphitheatre looking down on to the Seine. The church of Notre Dame was almost untouched by the June 1940 fire which raged through the town, virtually razing it. The adjacent houses have held up to this day to give some idea of what old Caudebec was like. Henri IV said of the 15th-century Notre Dame, an amazing flamboyant building, that it was the most beautiful chapel in the kingdom. However, it was the chapel of the Holy Sepulchre that inspired Fragonard to paint. It has some huge statues, allegedly purloined from nearby Jumièges Abbey. Even nearer and older is the next-door Saturday morning market, which goes back to 1390. There is also the near-obligatory Maritime Museum, this time devoted exclusively to the Seine navigation: its ports, its tradings, its shipbuilding and its fishing.

JUMIEGES

The ruins of this abbey are among the most famous and eye-catching in France. Built in the 7th century by St Philbert, it was razed by the Vikings, and the 10th-century rebuilding became known as the 'Jumièges almshouse' because of the charity of the occupants. The church was dedicated in 1067 with William the Conqueror himself looking on. It was nearly lost when a timber wallah had it in mind to bring it all down and work a stone quarry. Fifty years on he had still not had his way, and a new man restored the ruins to their present state. Much still stands, but only a small part of the lantern remains.

The *mascaret* or bore

Caudebec's main claim to fame during the past century has been the Seine *mascaret* (bore, aeger or aegre on the UK rivers Severn and Trent), which, before the advent of serious dredging and training, was a thing of wonder: to hear its approach was awesome, but to behold it clear and plain was breathtaking. The phenomenon used to be seen at its impressively dramatic height at Caudebec during the equinoctial tides. It is now seen less, being much diminished by the 'taming' work of engineering on the river banks. Although its effect is near to miraculous, its explanation is very straightforward: when big tides are running, the seas entering the estuary are funnelled between the river banks and, as they forge ahead, meet the normal river flow. Predictably, the power of the sea prevails, and immediately and amazingly reverses the stream, thus causing the mighty *mascaret*.

This is what I wrote about the Trent in my guide *Northeast Waterways*: 'Once upon a time, the Trent eagre (aegir, aegre, eager or bore) was a marvel and a wonder; a monster wall of implacable water making what seemed like a royal progress; that is, of Neptune seated on a hippocampus, overwhelming all before him. That is how I remember it as a boy being taken to witness its advance up the river from the banks just below Keadby bridge. That was more than fifty years ago and since then there have been training walls, draining schemes and massively engined coasters churning their way to Gainsborough, with the result that it is now little more than a token reminder of its former glorious but threatening self. Nevertheless, as I have had it put to me: 'It is not to be encountered broadsides on, standing in a dinghy.' If there is any chance that you are going to be involved in its path, make sure you take it straight on if under way, and if moored up slacken off your lines to give three or four feet extra slack, especially on your head rope. Nowadays, the eagre seldom exceeds a couple of feet, but in those times gone by it did get up to more than seven. This quite unusual and remarkable phenomenon is created by a combination of long, strong winds and an abnormally high spring tide. The already high tide is further impelled by the wind behind it until, as it floods up the narrowing river, it becomes the amazing surge that has been described as 'the forerunner of the Kraken waking' – and, most alarming to an impressionable child, it made a sound like that of the Titans organising themselves for battle.'

The *mascaret*, always arriving at LW, tends to form upstream of Caudebec when the tidal coefficient is more than 90. It is a non-breaking wall of water, between 1 and 1·5m high, moving at a speed that can reach 15 knots. The power of the sea surge is such that the direction of the current is immediately reversed and there is an equally sudden increase in water level. While it is no longer the threat it used to be, the *mascaret* is still a force to be reckoned with. Skippers should certainly stay with their craft, being ready to negotiate the swell and wash, and keeping well away not only from other vessels but also from immovable solid objects such as banks, jetties and quaysides.

In conclusion, I cannot do other than urge skippers to plan to make the trip to Rouen at one go. After a possibly sluggish start, getting to Honfleur for round about LW, the flood tide can be exploited all the way – and there will be nothing sluggish after that.

La Basse Seine – Rouen to Paris

If you need to take down masts and haven't done so in Le Havre, you must do so at Rouen. The local experts in this field are Lozai, at the Darse des Docks Flottants on the left bank at PK 251. See plan page 18. Demands are heavy, especially in the season, and it is advisable to get your booking in ahead (☎ 02 35 69 42 86). You could also try to arrange a short stay elsewhere, perhaps in the Darse Babin in the Bassin St-Gervais. Permission for this is obtained from the harbour office: moor at the Rouen port authority pontoon on the de Lesseps quay, upstream from the Bassin St-Gervais. Craft are usually allowed to stay there for a maximum of 48 hours, but most skippers and crew want to leave after 24. There are few domestic facilities nearby, and a late night trip to find a good but inexpensive restaurant or takeaway can be tedious.

Skippers with craft that can get under the bridges can proceed at once to the euphemistically described Pleasure Boat Harbour. This is just upstream of the Pont Corneille, and the pontoons are on the left bank of the right arm (the Bras du Pré-au-Loup branch). The pontoons have been improved over the past few years; there is now mains power and water, but they still leave much to be desired in stability and roping points. In general the authorities also leave you much alone. They are usually conspicuous by their absence when help is needed to tie up, but then, they do not unnecessarily pester you for money. They have been stating for nearly ten years now that vast improvements and fantastic refurbishments are 'in hand', but it must in any case be said that the mooring facility is by no means the least good or the worst value for money in France.

Good services and shops are available in the immediate vicinity, while all other things French that bring the visitor to the Seine are to be found on the north side in the major part of the city of Rouen itself. However, it is an energetic walk from the pontoons. From the boat at night, the brilliantly lit spire stands out, tempting photographers to do their best from unstable pontoons, demanding time for standing/ staring, and generally encouraging romantic perceptions. Undoubtedly Rouen is one of the most attractive and interesting cities in France, and I for one can find no fault with it.

Before departing, it is important to remember that traffic is permitted to move in the Bras du Pré-au-Loup only against the flow; that is, traffic proceeding upstream may do so only during (against) the ebb tide and traffic going downstream may do so only during (against) the flood.

ROUEN

Rouen, a good 60 miles from the sea, is somewhat surprisingly France's fifth busiest port, after Marseille, Le Havre, Dunkerque and Nantes-St-Nazaire; however, it is the first place on the river that is bridgeable, and that explains it all. The island of Lacroix was previously an industrial estate, but it is now a residential centre with many leisure amenities, including the marina. The north bank is the centre of Rouen today, but it is also still the headquarters of the *ancien régime*, with its old-city feel, historic towers and old restored houses; there are more than 700 of the classic half-timbered houses, in narrow streets. These consist of an oak framework with laths to infill and strengthen support, and a finishing fill of plaster. Just like many old houses in the county town of Lincolnshire, they are built to tolerate some subsidence and settlement; if desirable or necessary, they can be taken down and rebuilt elsewhere.

The cathedral, begun in the 12th century, is a splendid example of French Gothic, but its final form (after an original fire) did not take shape until the 16th century. It is interesting to note that Monet used one facade of the cathedral to paint the differing effects of light from sunrise to sunset.

However amazing it may be, it cannot compete for impact with the story of Joan of Arc. She was rehabilitated in 1456, but it was not until 1920 that she was canonised and made patron saint of France; there is now a splendid church on the site where she was put to death. She was questioned for three months, and after this fake trial she was burned alive on 30 May 1431 in the Place du Vieux Marché. English soldiers put her in a cart with a legend on her: 'Heretic – Apostate – Relapse – Idolatress'. It is said that her heart and entrails would not burn, so they were thrown, not to the dogs, but into the river. Some of the actual perpetrators and also some onlookers, perhaps tardily repenting, were heard to say that they would all burn in hell just as they had burned a saint.

It is not only today's footer-following, lager-louting herds that get us a bad name. In 15th-century Rouen our soldiers were known as Goddons, supposedly because of their liberal use of 'God Damned'.

Finding places to stop is no longer a serious problem after Rouen, and indeed there is one such on the right bank at PK 218, just over 20km upstream. It is the marina-type facility at Elbeuf, where things have improved dramatically. (Actually, the moorings are on the St-Aubin-les-Elbeuf side of the river, Elbeuf itself being on the left bank of the vast hairpin bend – an absolute classic in U-turns.) Restricting draught in the entrance and channel is now a good 2·5m, a whole metre better than it was not long ago, and access is no longer limited to ±2½ HW. It is not set in the most salubrious of surroundings, nor is it directly encompassed by a host of domestic or social facilities, but it is a very sheltered and secure haven with some boating services and access to mains power and water. Its backwater style (you need to weave a somewhat tortuous route through buoys and branches to reach the pontoons) makes for a quiet change from the life at Rouen.

The linked communities on both sides of the river form a largish conurbation. Some time ago, it was an important cloth-making town – some say, based on the skills of itinerant English cheats who absconded with plans and ideas from their north-country employers. Sheets were first made here in the 15th century, with the drapery business growing slowly until it was mechanised in the late 1980s. Commerce and industry are now more orientated to engineering.

The flamboyant church of St Stephen's in Elbeuf has much good stained glass; in particular, the Tree of Jesse and St Roch. True to its history, one of the panels shows drapers in their working attire. St John's Gothic church also has 16th-century stained glass, some actually going back to 1500, while to balance the feel there is also later and contemporary glass. The area has a natural history museum with a good display of local history. The nearby wooded park that commands the vicinity belonged to the Duke of Elbeuf – until the Revolution, that is.

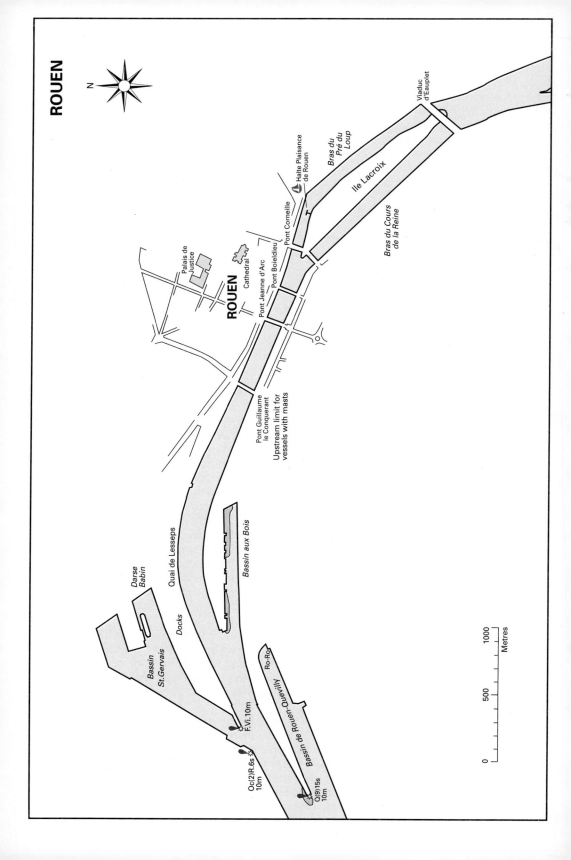

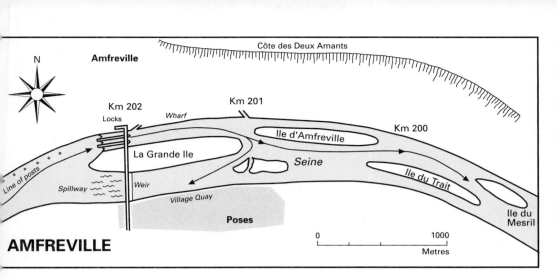

AMFREVILLE

Upstream from Elbeuf, the Seine gets progressively and dramatically more scenic, with magnificent cliffs, with every passing PK; not that every marker post is present, but it can be quite intriguing to catalogue them. In these stretches it has also narrowed to proportions that can unconditionally appeal to those for whom the sea has no serious attractions. The Seine is now becoming tamed – naturally, in its own way and in its own good time, on this last gasp of a leg, but more significantly in the factitious forms imposed by man: weirs and locks and training walls. Lovelace may well have been speaking 'as one having authority and not as the scribes' when he urged his pronouncement, 'Stone walls do not a prison make, Nor iron bars a cage', but that canon could in no way obtain when related to the masonry of the inland waterways of France. If even the mighty Rhône and Saône could be tamed by man, the Seine can have posed no problem when it was to be restrained and harnessed in the same manner.

The first and exemplary result of these near-Herculean labours comes at Les Ecluses d'Amfreville, just 16km after Elbeuf. On its last approaches to the lock the river Seine is not attractively scenic, and at low water it shows itself to be in need of care and protection, its banks partly collapsed and encumbered with much detritus, and its waters apparently (but perhaps only superficially) polluted if not indeed defiled. However, the situation improves somewhat just downstream of the lock, and very much more upstream of it. But before that joy and relaxation there is the question of the lock itself.

The Amfreville lock operators are extremely well-used to the antics of newcomers to their inland waterways, and have over the years adopted modi operandi and modi vivendi that seem able to accommodate most of the idiosyncrasies that boaters can demonstrate – including the intolerances of those argumentative Brits who feel that all Frenchmen should speak English. In general, the lock-keepers are friendly to a degree and cooperative to a point, and quite happily resigned to the problems that routinely accompany the passage of leisure craft. However, their operation can be a 90-minute long-winded assignment, so it is best to be prepared for a delay and pleased if the wait is only brief. Like most lock-keepers (and many French folk at large), they have an enduring penchant for all things laid back and a peculiar talent for expressing that attitude through body language that relies essentially on the raising of shoulders and eyebrows allied with a flamboyant outspreading of hands: all in all, expressive body language that can hardly be missed or misunderstood. In the event, the lock is handleable and the keepers are pliable; there is no hint of threat or unpleasantness, and the experience is usually perceived by experienced English canal users as an improvement on things back home.

The River Seine from sea to source 25

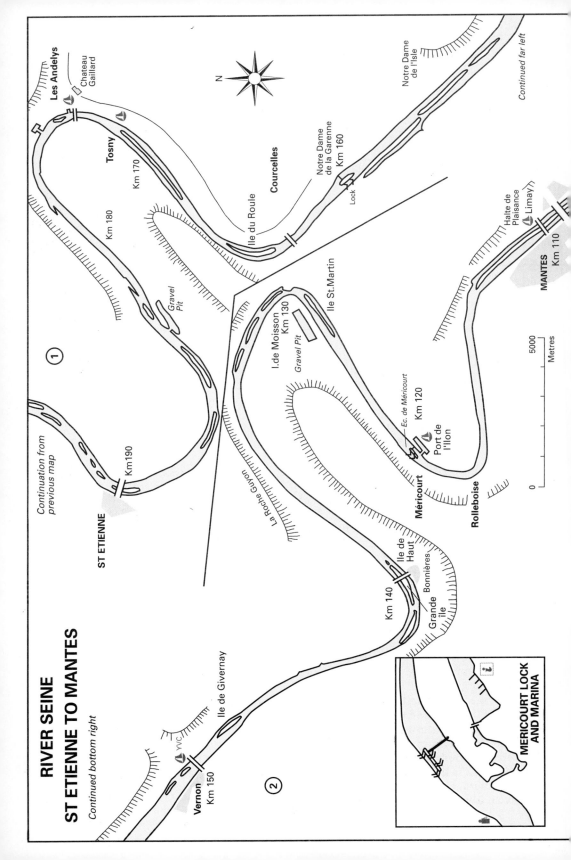

RIVER SEINE
ST ETIENNE TO MANTES

Continued bottom right

Continuation from
previous map

ST ETIENNE

Km190

Km 180

Les Andelys

Chateau
Gaillard

Tosny

Km 170

Ile du Roule

Gravel
Pit

Courcelles

Notre Dame
de la Garenne
Km 160

Lock

Notre Dame
de l'Isle

Continued far left

N

Halte de
Plaisance

Limay

MANTES

Km 110

I.de Moisson
Km 130

Ile St.Martin

Gravel Pit

Ec. de Méricourt
Km 120

Port de
l'Ilon

Méricourt

Rolleboise

La Roche Guyon

Ile de
Haut

Bonnières

Grande
Île

Km 140

Ile de Givernay

VVC

Vernon
Km 150

5000

Metres

0

1

2

MERICOURT LOCK
AND MARINA

Poseurs the lock-keepers certainly are not, but there are plenty of poses to be found by the lock and its upstream islands. They are part of a community of poses: le Port de Poses, le Bas de Poses, le Mesnil de Poses, and, just for good measure, Poses itself. Together, they combine to offer an intriguing and restful stop after what may have been a tiring or even demanding trip up the tidal Seine. All basics can be found in the nearby shops, and there is a café/bar immediately next the lock. Bankside moorings are available all around and the atmosphere is as peaceful and quiet as you could wish. You can put your stakes in the green banks and stay away from it all, or try for a wall on the left bank nearer the village and have someone to talk to all the livelong day. I have never met an unfriendly soul in Poses.

Now comes a quite sudden and dramatic change in the landscape of the Seine. It would be untrue to say that 'Earth has not anything to show more fair', but perfectly valid to claim 'Dull would he be of soul who could pass by a sight so ...' changed in its particulars. It really does seem that 'The river glideth at his own sweet will' – and all that lies ahead is the promising mighty heart of a river inviting friendly exploration. For those who know the northeast waterways of the UK, I would liken the changes on passing through the lock here to those to be experienced at Naburn on the Yorkshire Ouse, where one moves from the broken-down rural rough and tumble of the tidal stretch into the milk and honey lawns of the rich refugees from the nearby city of York.

Moving upstream, there are one-way traffic schemes to be followed: they are obvious and in any case well marked. The current in these non-tidal waters averages 1·8km/h in summer, but it can reach more when the winter to spring snow and rain do their stuff. Above Amfreville there are frequent elongated islands (islets or *îlots* as in Thames eyots or aits), the ends of which project far out as (usually unmarked) shoals up and downstream for up to 200m, and there is also a great deal of detritus, which lurks just below the surface.

Ahead lie some really choice backwaters affording sanctuary from the world at large. Many have very good depths, and some have their draught posted at the commencement of the arm or leg; nevertheless, it is always best to keep one eye on the sounder – and another on the banks for debris, garbage, broken wooden poles and fallen concrete posts. With caution, the whole of the long arm that appears to port after the last of the Poses, namely le Mesnil, can be negotiated until it joins the main stream again just before Porte Joie at PK 194. It may be possible to talk or arm-twist your way on to a 24-hour stop at one of the private quay/moorings by the small town. If not, there are more similar choices immediately ahead: to port for the shallower channel (which can shoal to 1·2m in places but is generally OK for 1·5m) and another collection of private possibilities at St-Pierre du Vauvray, PK 191. After a slightly broader run of 7km there comes a supposedly welcoming yacht club, but in reality its appearance, from entry onwards, is as off-putting as its welcome is lukewarm. Better to move on to the much more appealing proposition of the mini Port de Plaisance at Les Andelys, only another 10km. Before you reach it, you pass the small yacht club Paris-Normandie on the right bank, with a depth which can reach 1·5m. There is seldom much room or much of a welcome for a visitor, but then why should there be when there are the facilities of Les Andelys awaiting visitors only just upstream?

'Port de Plaisance des Andelys', proclaims the legend. In fact it is merely a small basin, but while that is exactly true, it is not the whole truth, for there is much to be found that is as large as life and big-hearted in this little harbour. To get in, you need to negotiate a dogleg entrance which is also encumbered by a number of small buoys. As a result there is little room to manoeuvre. On the plus side, the alongside and stern-to pontoon facilities have been improved. The basin has been dredged to nearly 2m, and mains power and water are now in good working order.

Once you are in – you are in. The informal harbour staff (apparently a family) are friendly and helpful, and not at all speedy or even demanding when it comes to bring-

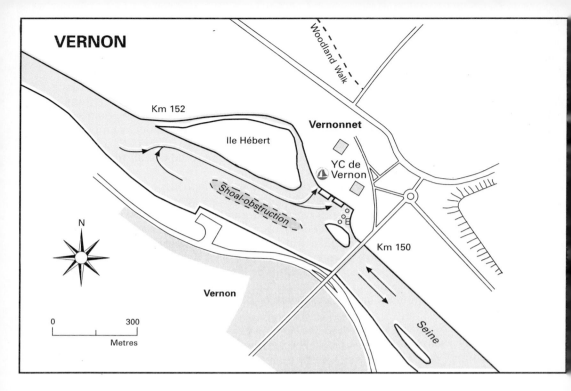

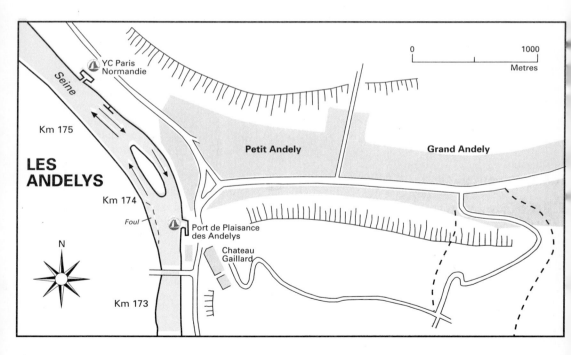

ing the bill. (There are those who prefer to stay on the cheap and lie to the piles out-side. True, you pay nothing in cash, but the price in anxiety prompted by the move-ments of barges – close to and closer still – cannot be worth the few FF that are saved.) The marina is overlooked by the splendour of the Château Gaillard atop its precipitous small mountain, while at river level only a few minutes' walk away are all the facilities of what is a most attractive village with good shopping. This is a pleasant haven with a pleasing ambience.

LES ANDELYS

Andely comes in two parts: Petit Andely to the west and Grand Andely to the east. While most boaters know about Château Gaillard because it is almost impossible to miss its fantastic silhouette when coming up the river, not so many know of the 6th-century Clotilde monastery in Grand Andely. She was the wife of Clovis and has a street named after her. In it there is a fountain where she (allegedly) turned water into wine for the chapel workers.

Château Gaillard itself is an amazing fortress originally consisting of two parts: the main fort, high above the river, and the forward redoubt across the moat with its five towers, of which the tallest is still intact. If you follow the wall round you can see the keep foundations, which 'grow' straight from nature's rocks. There is a notice about the dangers of falling brickwork, but that is not the only hazard, for you need to be more than sound in wind and limb to succeed in the demanding climb that faces you on an ascent from the marina.

Take heed of the following tale. Baron Rulph lived here with his beautiful daugh-ter, Calixte. She was rescued one day from the clutches of a wild pig by her lover Edmond. The Wicked Baron wanted to reward Edmond a bit – but not a lot – so was confounded when he asked to marry her. The Baron Rulph gave his conditional ap-proval: conditional upon Edmond climbing the hill three times with Calixte on his back. Edmond succeeded, arriving at the top for the third time only to drop dead. Calixte, who had an eye for a tragic scenario, picked up the dead Edmond and hurled herself with him in her arms off the cliff. You have been warned.

Every year, the nearby town has what must be the most amazing car boot sale in France. Towards the end of September, the whole place is taken over by stallholders from the huge to the minuscule: some work in teams of three or four, unloading giant pantechnicons, literally broadcasting their wares, while at the other end of the spec-trum one little old lady is selling one old vase from its isolated position on one old chair. Unforgettable.

Just over a couple of kilometres upstream on the left bank is the small community of Tosny. At first glance the small arm of the river seems attractive, but exploration shows that there is little water except in the middle of the channel. Close inspection shows there to be nowhere on the bankside to moor or even just tie up your boat, that is if you could get it there without touching bottom in the first place.

After a wide stretch of 10km from Tosny comes the next lock, Notre Dame de la Garenne (also known as yet another Château Neuf). Its huge barrage and hydro-elec-tric station are to port. In front of the barrage is a collection of stones, rocks, poles and stakes, usually well marked by an assortment of sentinel shags.

Three kilometres upstream, just after PK 158 on the right bank, by the small set-tlement of Notre Dame de l'Isle, there is another long deviation, fairly wide and deep, that encompasses the three islands Emien, Souquet and La Madeleine (also called La Souveraine). Just into the deviation there is a small boatyard, but I have never seen signs of boating or engineering life there. It has pontoons, but they are not a stable system and do not appear to be serviced in any way at all. It could be useful in an emergency, but is otherwise of no interest. On the main drag there are also quayside piles and moorings, of which the same must be said. In general, the area is run down and does not call out for exploration. Better it must be to move up to PK 150 and the twinned towns of Vernon (left bank) and Vernonnet (right bank).

Just below the bridge by the Ile Hébert there are shoal waters on the northerly side of the centre channel. They also surround this island and the other (unnamed) closer to the bridge. This latter is virtually connected to the piles of the bridge, which is topped by an aged, ageing timbered house. Between the two islands, almost hidden away in a near-backwater, are the pontoons of the yacht club. The pontoons carry little water and there is shoal water all round ... definitely an area where caution is to be exercised. Immediately upstream of the bridge, on the left bank, there is a small pontoon facility in an area much used by speed and ski merchants. The approach area is buoyed; upstream there is an island, followed by a permanent ski ramp. This pontoon has the merit of being on the right side of the tracks, for the yacht club itself is across the river from the main town.

It is a pity that Vernon does not have more facilities for visitors, since it is an interesting place to explore, especially the old castle dungeon, the Château de Bizy of Louis XV and Louis-Philippe, and the Claude Monet museum, in Monet's house.

After another 10km comes a further broad reach with accompanying arms and islands. The area can be navigated with caution, as the depths vary from better than 4m to not so good as 1·2m. This leads us to Bonnière-sur-Seine and the Grande Ile. There is a channel between the island and the right bank, but although it starts off quite deep, it soon loses water, dropping to 1·2m at best. It is prudent, therefore, to leave the island to port and keep in the main channel. Once under the bridge and past the two small 'promontory' islands, you have to look back to see the modest pontoon facilities of the small boatyards. As at Vernonnet, they are almost hidden away, but here it is not possible to see them until you have actually steamed right past. Here also, they are on the 'other' side of the river from the main town, actually in the suburb of Gloton.

LA ROCHE-GUYON

After the islands, just over 5km along a broad reach, comes La Roche-Guyon on the right bank at PK 133. There are small pontoons here belonging to the local yacht club, and it is just possible to talk your way in – especially if your French is up to convincing the indigens that you are a true seeker after culture and enlightenment, for this is one of the most prestigious *châteaux* in the whole of the country. Its gates carry the famous arms of the Rochefoucauld family.

Perhaps due attention to two of the maxims of the 17th-century Duc de la Rochefoucauld may pay dividends: 'To establish oneself in the world one has to do all one can to appear established'; and 'Anything may happen in France.'

The village started life in the 13th century as a small stronghold with a *château* at the foot of the cliff linked to the keep by rocky steps. La Roche-Guyon was made a duchy peerage in 1621, and just over half a century later it went to La Rochefoucauld, many of whose epigrams were penned here. In 1816 Louis-François Auguste took over, and here he entertained Victor Hugo, Lamartine and others. In 1829 he sold the *château* back to the Rochefoucaulds, and it has been in the family ever since.

The place is said to have inspired Zola, not the greatest of sentimental romantics, to pen the following: 'and they also had the river, taking to it like wild savages, living entire days there, sailing, discovering new lands, remaining hidden beneath weeping willows, in narrows dark with shade. Going with the stream, between a scattering of islands, there was a whole mysterious township in motion, alleys criss-crossing down which they gently ambled, lightly caressed by low branches, alone in a world of woodpigeons and kingfishers ... he often took a slow walk along the Seine, without ever straying further than a kilometre.'

After the near isolation that can be felt at some of the modest pontoons found (sometimes with a welcoming proprietor) on the banks along these broad reaches, the lock at Méricourt and the marina just after it offer a pleasant change. The Méricourt lock is a smooth and friendly experience, with plenty of good bankside moorings for those who just want a short break. As at many of the approaches to the locks where there are good long bankside waiting areas, by arrangement with the lock-keeper you can moor overnight.

Actually, the marina known as Port de l'Ilon is only 50km from Andelys and makes a pleasantly easy leg for those who wish not to dally but equally do not want to be rushed. To approach the marina, you steam straight past the island on the port hand that keeps you away from the Ile de Sablonnière, the shoaled stretch upstream of the barrage. Once past this 'island', you turn hard to port and go slightly downstream – only slightly, otherwise you will be making for the barrage itself. The entrance to the marina does have a legend announcing its presence, but both are pretty well hidden away until you get close. The entry is not wide and the route is pleasantly tortuous, through the tree-surrounded 'lakes' left behind from previous lives long gone. Eventually the large water opens up and the marina shows itself quite clearly. All 'no-go' areas are well marked by buoys – but they are well-distanced from the channel to the berths. Visitors are generally welcomed to an outer pontoon.

The setup is calm, quiet and friendly, in spite of the fact that the marina has very substantial boat-building, repairing and engineering enterprises on site. However, although the boating side of the marina is first class, there are few facilities for domestics and socialising. The usual toiletries are present, and from time to time the payphone will work, but for the other ordinary basics of living you need to arrive with full rations or be prepared to take a trip in the dinghy across the river to the small community of Rolleboise, where it is also possible to obtain yacht fuel from the riverside station. Port de l'Ilon is an inexpensive, ideal spot if you want nothing more than a good rest away from almost everything but nature.

We are now not many kilometres over a hundred from Paris, and the surroundings slowly begin to reflect the change in atmosphere, as just over 10km upstream we approach the twinned towns of Mantes la Jolie on the left bank and Limay on the right bank at PK 110. All the cruising facilities are to be found on the Limay side, and it can be approached via the Bras de Limay, which has 4m all through. The boatyards in this area are not in the first league; indeed, some of their facilities do not get into a league of any kind, and it is far better to try for the Halte de Plaisance de Limay, which is to be found just below the bridge (Pont de Mantes) in the Bras de Limay. It is far superior, and, what is more, better placed for easy access to the shops and banks. The two major islands are known as Limay and L'Aumone, but there is more: the upstream end of L'Aumone is known as the Ile aux Boeufs, while the downstream extremity of Limay has been eulogised, perhaps, with the cognomen Ile aux Dames. Although I asked at great length, no-one was able to cast light on what I found an extraordinary confrontation of appellations. The Halte de Plaisance faces the ladies.

Limay is really a suburb of Mantes, joined to it Siamese style by the umbilical of the Pont de Mantes. Each has an important church: the smaller one at Limay is all 12th century, while the larger Gothic Notre Dame in Mantes was erected from the 12th to the 15th. The painter Corot was much inspired by the Notre Dame in Mantes la Jolie.

The next hospitable stop comes at Meulan, just under 20km from Limay. There are two routes for quitting the Halte: going back downstream to the small channel between the Dames and the Boeufs and then into the main arm, avoiding the downstream silting on the main headland of the island as you round the corner to port, or continuing upstream to meet the main river again at the end of the Ile de Limay. Here, as you turn, you need to respect the red and green buoys marking the entrance to the Daniel Dreyfous Ducas Darse and the extrusion of detritus and silt from the upstream headland of the island. When crossing between the two, it is possible just to touch on the soft bottom of an incipient bar that reaches across. It is of no serious concern unless you are drawing more than 2m.

The Seine is now a major traffic highway again, having left behind most of its rural miniatures. They will not really be regained until it becomes the Petit Seine, past Montreau. Here, en route for Paris, which for centuries represented the height of erotic temptation and the depth of sexual cupidity for many tight-lipped Englishmen, the waterway is broad. Perhaps Matthew's words may be apposite, if not apostolic, here: 'Wide is the gate, and broad is the way, that leadeth to destruction, and many there be which go in thereat.'

However, our first port of call is no fleshpot, being the small community of Meulan at PK 93, just past the old Mureaux lock. In fact you may not pass it at all, for there are again islands to be negotiated on this stretch. First, just over 5km from Limay, is the chunky Ile La Ville (known as Ile de Rangiport), around which traffic is directed one way only. It is just over a kilometre in length. Another 2km upstream brings another island, this one long and thin at well over 5km. You can take either arm to reach the Halte de Plaisance de Meulan. The main reach, the Bras des Mureaux, is to starboard with the old lock on the left bank at PK 95, while the minor arm, the Bras de Mezy, is to port. It may be the smaller of the two, but it still carries between 3m and 4m almost to the end of the main island. This 'main' island, in fact, like Caesar's Gaul, ' ... est omnia divisa in partes tres'; the three parts are first de Juziers, second de Mezy, and third Belle Ile. However, the quotation is not absolutely apt, since there is a sort of disclaimer of an island at the upstream extremity: Le Fort, round which there are two named channels when the Bras de Mezy splits to encompass it. They are the Bras St-Come and the Bras de Meulan. Logically for once the French have got it right, putting the Halte de Meulan in the Bras de Meulan – a feat which must have caused consternation in those camps still stubbornly wedded to the concept of idiosyncratic Gallic caprices and things whimsical.

The Halte de Meulan is kept in clean working order; since it is, predictably, popular, it is good to know that there are further possibilities of mooring at the banksides when the pontoon is fully occupied. In addition, it is well placed for the centre of what is an utterly charming small town, with an excellent shopping centre and a very good open-air market – which is only footsteps away from the mooring.

After Meulan, the words of the Marquise de Pompadour come to mind: 'Après nous le deluge', insofar as the 20km stretch of the Seine to the next lock at Andresy is positively littered with boatyards and pontoons. This proliferation is a new experience on the Seine, but unfortunately they are of little appeal and even less use, since most are too small, too shoal or too exclusively private (or privately exclusive) for cruising Brits. However, there are one or two specials to look out for. Just over a couple of kilometres after Meulan comes a long island to port on the north bank side: this is the Ile de Vaux, and it carries good water all along its mainland channel. There used to be a restaurant with a small pontoon, and there have been promises that it will be open again. The route is a not unattractive alternative to the main arm. Over the next 6km to the end of the large island pair (Ile d'Hernière and Ile de Medan, separated by a narrow unnavigable channel) there are many good restaurants, each with its sound pontoon for patrons. There is also a working boatyard just before the bridge near PK 85. After this bridge, the Pont de Triel, both arms round the islands are navigable: the Bras de Medan and the Bras des Mottes. The whole area is busy in a new kind of way, indicating the proximity of the capital and the need for commuter-type leisure facilities. There is also a working ferry on the Melun arm.

Just after the two channels rejoin, between the Ile de Meulan and the Ile de Villennes on the port hand just at PK 81 is the pretentiously named Port de Plaisance de Port St-Louis. It is a disaster of a broken-down affair with neither facilities nor welcome. Should you be unhappy enough to be caught out and put in a berth, extortionate fees may well be demanded. Far better it is to steam past the many islands on both hands straight up to the Andresy lock and the confluence with the river Oise. There are boatyards en route, some nearly hidden away, but some really big ones, specialising in building and repairing *péniches*.

The lock at Andresy is a busy one and you are not likely to be kept waiting. In common with other keepers of busy locks in France, the Andresy lock-keepers do not deem it necessary to answer VHF calls from leisure craft, so any notice of arrival or request for opening you make may well receive no response. Their silence in no way indicates anything other than absence of speaking: you will be passed through in a most friendly and efficient manner.

Once through the lock we arrive at a most important junction. It is here that the rivers Oise and Seine meet and merge, with the two large barge communities of Andresy and Conflans Ste Honorine respectively on the west and east banks of the Oise and both on the north bank of the Seine. Should you want a break at this stage, you will be spoilt for choice. There are five possibilities: the Halte de Plaisance at Andresy in its quiet backwater, the new Mediterranean-style marina at Cergy Pontoise (10km up the Oise), the packed and busy-to-bursting right-bank quaysides and barges at Conflans Ste Honorine, the left-bank Ambiance Yachting small boatyard just past Conflans at PK 69, and the small Halte de Plaisance de la Frette on the right bank at PK 62.

The main channel to the Andresy lock is known as the Bras de Plafosse. It is separated from the north mainland by two islands: Ile de la Derivation and Ile d'En Bas. What used to be a navigable arm, the Bras d'Andresy, is no longer so, being blocked by the old Carrières-sous-Poissy lock and the barrage between the two islands. To reach the pontoon at Andresy you round the headland of the second island, the Ile d'En Bas, at a good 20m and make a hairpin bend into what is now in essence a backwater. You pass the barge park and trip-boat jetty on the north bank and the Halte will then shortly appear to starboard, with its five mooring buoys on the island side to port.

Andresy is a small well knit community with all basic services. Everybody seems to know everybody, a fact that is amply demonstrated at the splendid Saturday market, which is held on the river bank. The pontoon (with mains power and water usually working) is on a quiet section of road just behind the police substation and a public telephone kiosk. Bars and cafés are close by, but the nearest eating house is perhaps the most tempting: a small but splendid Moroccan restaurant.

The second choice, the new Mediterranean-style marina at Cergy Pontoise, is 10km up the Oise and well worth the detour. (For more information on Cergy, please turn to the section on the river Oise at page 55.)

Nearby Conflans Ste Honorine has almost everything except peace and space; it certainly has plenty of confusion and noise. Its quaysides and walls and barges always appear to proffer a warm welcome, but it is only the warmth that is real: it is a hollow welcome for visitors when there is no room at the inn. However, luck could be in your favour; even in the absence of a hole in the wall, you might find a barge that is expecting neither to leave in the middle of the night nor to receive another working barge to raft up any minute. Twenty-four hours could be yours – and such a spell in Conflans is well worth the search.

There are residual signs of and for Ambiance Yachting a kilometre past their present site and on the opposite (the right) bank. They merely indicate a glory that perhaps once was, since there are also signs proclaiming that it is dangerous to approach, let alone to moor. Nowadays it is a modest working marina and boatyard. It is on the other side of the river from the town and all its facilities, but there are basic services in the marina and it is a quiet spot. Ambiance has an ambience of quietly disorganised industry in the middle of quietly almost-unspoiled countryside.

The last of the quinary is the diminutive Halte at La Frette, just over 5km upstream from Ambiance on the right bank at PK 62. It is well hidden away among the trees;

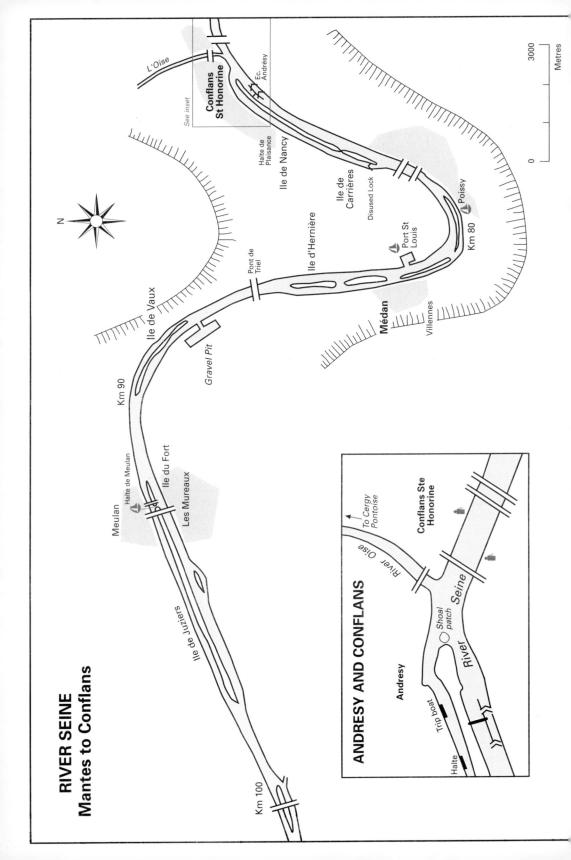

RIVER SEINE
Mantes to Conflans

N

Km 100

Ile de Juziers

Meulan

Halte de Meulan

Ile du Fort

Les Mureaux

Km 90

Ile de Vaux

Gravel Pit

Pont de Triel

Ile d'Hernière

Ile de Carrières

Port St Louis

Disused Lock

Médan

Villennes

Km 80

Poissy

Ile de Nancy

Halte de Plaisance

L'Oise

Conflans St Honorine

Ec. Andrésy

See inset

0

3000

Metres

ANDRESY AND CONFLANS

Andresy

To Cergy Pontoise

River Oise

Conflans Ste Honorine

Shoal patch

River Seine

Trip boat

Halte

so well that you can easily steam past it without seeing a thing. It sits quietly under the trees, while up above the world goes by on the busy main road. There is, however, a public telephone kiosk and an excellent wine cellar, and its mains services have been known to work.

All these locations are first rate in their own way. You pays your money (or not, as the case may be) and you takes your choice: Andresy and La Frette are completely free, Conflans usually is, Ambiance is inexpensive, that is if they actually take your money at all, and Cergy takes full whack for its finesse, giving value for your liquid assets. We will return to a cruise of the river Oise later.

CONFLANS STE HONORINE

This barge centre sits at the confluence of the Oise to the north and the Seine to the east and west. River traffic comes virtually from all over Europe. Not as much now, true; and there are far too many empty barges awaiting commissions that will probably never materialise. Conflans Ste Honorine has every right to call itself the French Bargees' Capital.

Conflans was an important staging post for towing: sometimes 40 hands were needed to pull a boat upstream, the current being so fierce. In olden days, coal-barges were brought down the Oise by horses to muster up a '15-train convoy' for the tow to Paris, when they were in the hands of steam-driven winches and the laid chain on the river bed. The arrival of propellers eliminated the chains. But those days are gone, and single-handed bargees or three-crew diesel pushers have taken all the work.

All the bargees liked Conflans, and the Conflans folk liked them: it was a symbiosis. You could walk along the old towpath to the Ambiance Yachting boatyard and inspect the craft of the wealthy from next-door Maisons-Lafitte. Ambiance Yachting is still there, but is now nearly hidden on the opposite bank, while its original yard is overgrown and has dangerous overhangs and pilings on the river edge. So pass all things.

Once the anomie of the conurbation of mainly unemployed barges at Conflans has been left behind, the river opens wide again and proceeds, at an apparently leisurely pace through surroundings that cannot be described as specially graceful, to Bougival, some 20km ahead. In spite of the wondrous lifestyles of the fashion followers of Maison-Lafitte and the trendsetters of St-Germain en Laye, to say nothing of the fleshpots of the Hippodromes, I found the scenes as viewed from the river less astounding (or even outstanding) than I had been led to expect.

Just past PK 53, there is the large Ile Corbière and the railway bridge of Pont du Pecq to be avoided. (Note its keep-right one-way traffic system.) All this should be carefully observed well ahead of time, since some of the barges that motor along with more than a little alacrity can approach and leave at unexpected angles. Otherwise, it is broadly on to where the navigation splits into two, offering a choice of routes: the river Neuve or the Marly arm. I have always taken the advice of the Bougival lock-keepers, who recommend the Marly stretch for leisure craft. This arm is reached through the Bougival lock itself. The Neuve leads to the Chatou lock but has no stopping place or amenities for cruising folk. On the Marly line there are two Haltes and a splendid new yacht club pontoon. The first Halte is no more than a kilometre after the lock on the port hand. I was intrigued by coming across various mentions of Bougival as being an old haunt of Impressionist painters, and that was enough to send me in search of painterly culture. Having crossed a terrifying road traffic bridge I unearthed a splendid photographic museum and a huge proliferation of shops. The Halte is convenient for the town, but is also noisy from road traffic, and busy with barges first and last thing. It shares a drawback with the next (Chatou) Halte: both are popular with live-aboards who are permanently plugged into the mains power and water supplies, so that some determination is required to get your fair share. On more than one occasion I have had to resort to unplugging some leads physically when even

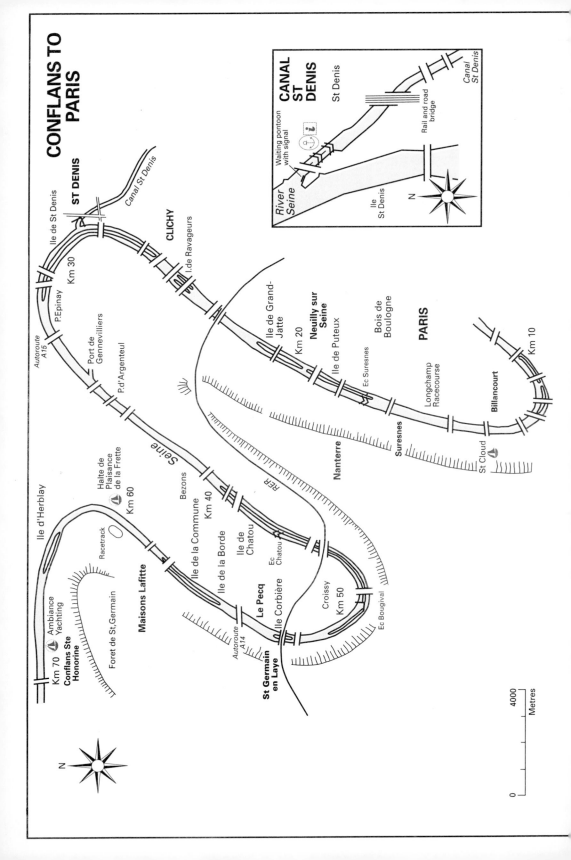

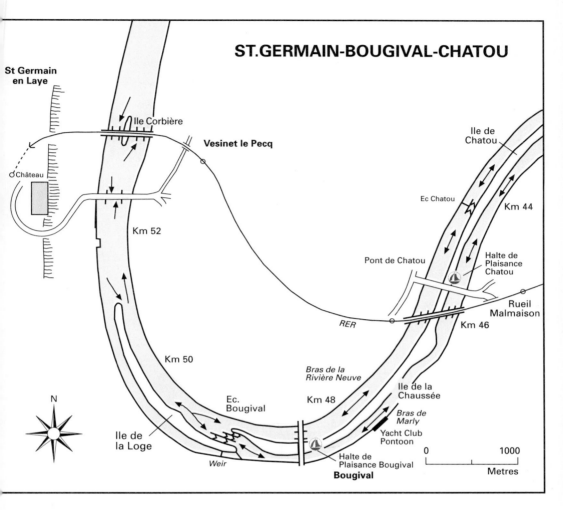

ST.GERMAIN-BOUGIVAL-CHATOU

St Germain en Laye

Ile Corbière

Vesinet le Pecq

Château

Km 52

Ile de Chatou

Ec Chatou

Km 44

Pont de Chatou

Halte de Plaisance Chatou

Rueil Malmaison

RER

Km 46

Km 50

N

Bras de la Rivière Neuve

Km 48

Ile de la Chaussée

Bras de Marly

Ec. Bougival

Yacht Club Pontoon

Ile de la Loge

Weir

Halte de Plaisance Bougival

Bougival

0   1000

Metres

repeated threats of summoning the police did not have their usual effect. It is to be hoped that the French authorities will keep their promise to tighten up on those boaters who exploit the system. An undesirable feature of an otherwise very desirable residence.

BOUGIVAL

In the 1800s Bougival was the vibrant centre of the Parisian dolce vita, and life was lived as if Ars Longa Vita Brevis meant Art Today, Heart Attack Tomorrow. Corot and Bizet lived here, and the floating yuppies of the day were celebrated by Renoir and Maupassant. The exiled Turgenev also lived here, and in the house museum are some of his papers and photographs, his piano and a recreation of the room in which he died in 1883.

Looking for a quieter life will take you to the extremely well made private pontoon near the restaurant just after PK 48. The pontoon belongs to a local yacht club with a clientele affluent enough to be able to afford the near-exorbitant prices of the riverside eating house. The club members are retiring: only once have I been visited by them – and they were extremely welcoming.

The final resting place is the Chatou Halte, ironically not sited on the Chatou lock

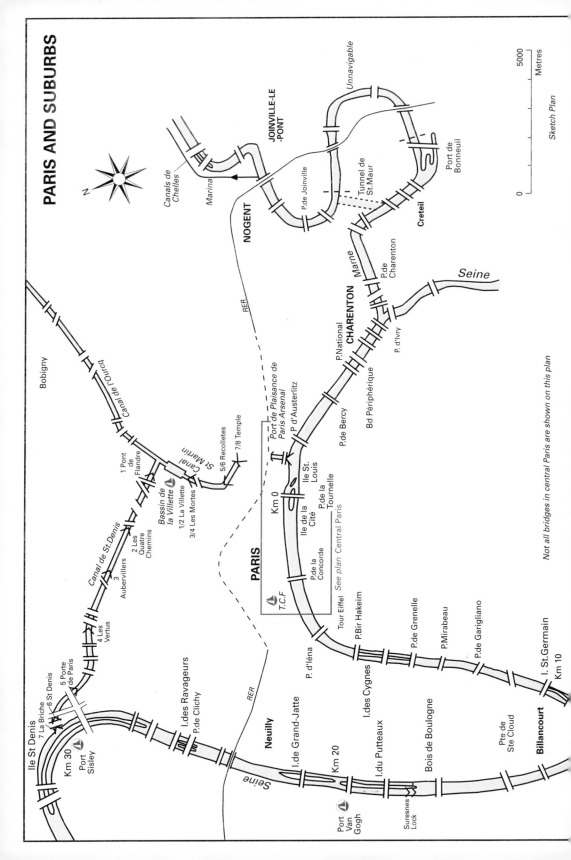

PARIS AND SUBURBS

Sketch Plan

Metres
5000
0

Not all bridges in central Paris are shown on this plan

N

PARIS

See plan Central Paris

Km 0

T.C.F

Seine

Neuilly

RER

RER

Ile St Denis
Km 30
Port Sisley
7 La Briche
6 St Denis
5 Porte de Paris
4 Les Vertus
3 Aubervilliers
2 Les Quatre Chemins
1 Pont de Flandre
Canal de St.Denis
Canal de l'Ourcq
Bobigny

I.des Ravageurs
P.de Clichy

Bassin de la Villette
1/2 La Villette
3/4 Les Mortes
5/6 Recolletes
7/8 Temple
Canal St.Martin

Port Van Gogh
Suresnes Lock
I.de Grand-Jatte
Km 20
I.du Putteaux
Bois de Boulogne
Pte de Ste Cloud

Port de Plaisance de Paris Arsenal
P.d'Austerlitz
Ile de la Cité
Ile St. Louis
P.de la Tournelle
P.de la Concorde
Tour Eiffel
P.Bir Hakeim
P. d'Iéna
I.des Cygnes
P.de Grenelle
P.Mirabeau
P.de Garigliano
I. St.Germain
Km 10
Billancourt

P.de Bercy
Bd Périphérique
P.National
CHARENTON
Marne
P.de Charenton
P. d'Ivry
Seine

Creteil
Port de Bonneuil
Tunnel de St.Maur
P.de Joinville
Marina
JOINVILLE-LE-PONT
NOGENT
Canals de Chelles
Unnavigable

arm at all. It is similar to the one at Bougival insofar as it is near big-town facilities and lots of noise. At 45km from Paris, we are now well within an easy day's cruising. Two routes lie ahead after the first 10km. The river route goes with the Seine all the way, while the other branches off at the Dark-Arches entrance into the definitely nether regions of the Canal St-Martin. While offering very contrasting approaches to the city centre, they will both eventually let you rest in what is probably the best-known marina on the Seine: the Port de Plaisance de Paris Arsenal – or the Bastille. The Seine takes you in at the front door, while St-Martin guides you through the back.

The two arms of the river become reunited at PK 40 and we continue broadly on past the commercial docks on the left bank that stretch for a good couple of kilometres. The split for the canal/river route does not come until PK 33, where we meet the famous Ile St-Denis. The entrance to the canal is 3km up the port side; that is, leaving the Ile St-Denis to starboard. We will return to the canal later – please see below at page 42.

THE RIVER ROUTE TO THE BASTILLE

Both routes round the 8km-long island lead to Paris, but only the northerly channel goes to the canal entrance. The other arm continues on its commerce-surrounded way and the two do not join up again until just after PK 26. There are lots of free mooring possibilities on this route. Few are organised or have any proper facility for leisure craft, and few offer what might be called secure and friendly berths. Just by PK 29 is Port Sisley, where there is what can only be described as a basic marina-cum-mooring facility. I have never been enamoured of this spot, and while I have never come to harm here, I always feel anxious. I have actually met some skippers who have had to fend off burgling intruders afloat, and others who have spent a sleepless night thanks to the discordant hullabaloo from parties ashore and afloat. All in all the area is industrial and dismally so. For those who want to moor in something like comfort without going into the Paris Arsenal, there is a fairly new, fairly posh establishment at PK 24, just two kilometres after the upstream end of the island. Known as Port Van Gogh, it has quite a few very obvious berths for very large craft, while those for smaller boats (10–12m) are hidden away ... as are frequently all members of staff. Once you have searched them out, or they have found you, they are extremely friendly, and it is a clean and well serviced spot. Other than the marina itself, comprehensive socialising and domestic facilities are fairly distant. You may get charged a lot to stay – or you may get off free.

In no time after Van Gogh we are at Suresnes, the last of the locks before the centre of Paris. It is the classic large, old-fashioned type, with crumbling brickwork, slimy walls and the very best in amiable keepers. I have neither experienced nor observed an unfriendly incident here. It is just under 20km to Notre Dame, and French/Seine river life now begins in earnest. For comment we might just adjust Tennyson: 'On either side the river are, Long streets of concrete and of tar, That line the routes with cab and car; And thro the town the stream runs far, To many splendoured Notre Dame.'

On a more serious note, pondering L'Inconnue de la Seine, his words are tellingly appropriate and sadly fitting: 'He said, "She has a lovely face; God in his mercy lend her grace, The Lady of Shalott."' Indeed, the last time I saw Paris, just having passed Notre Dame, in fact, it was to observe a dead soul being enclosed in a body bag, having just been dragged from the river in the very same way at the very same spot.

From here on, there are lots of potential stopping places for small boats on the banks of the Seine, among them the well known but not so well appointed Port de Champs Elysées and the Touring Club de France. They are usually very friendly – but equally usually very full. It must be said of all the river moorings, prestigious club or common wall, that they are no good if you cannot easily tolerate the noise of

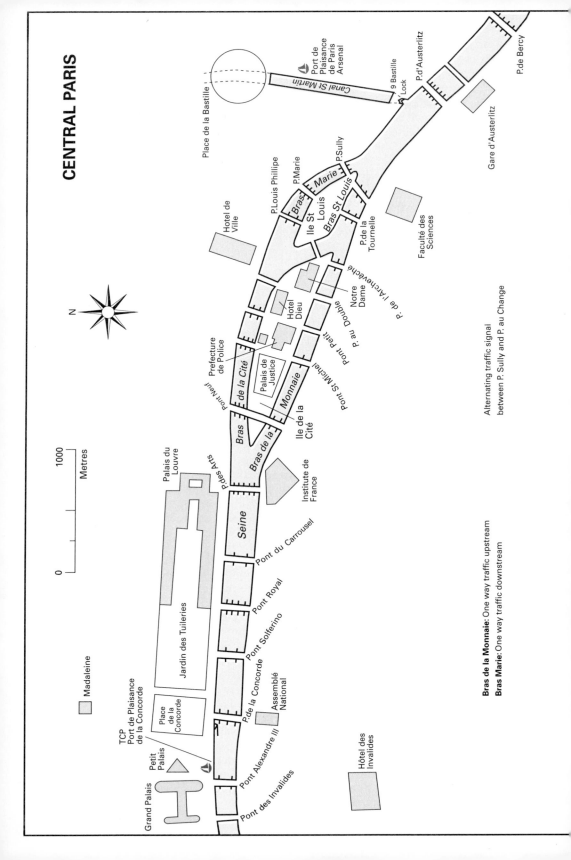

CENTRAL PARIS

N

Metres
0   1000

Madeleine

TCP Port de Plaisance de la Concorde

Petit Palais

Grand Palais

Palais du Louvre

Jardin des Tuileries

Place de la Concorde

P. de la Concorde

Assemblé National

Pont Alexandre III

Pont des Invalides

Hôtel des Invalides

Pont Solferino

Pont Royal

Pont du Carrousel

Seine

P. des Arts

Institute de France

Bras de la Seine

Bras de la Monnaie

Ile de la Cité

Pont Neuf

Prefecture de Police

Palais de Justice

Pont St.Michel

p. au Double

Pont Petit

P. de l'Archevêché

Notre Dame

Hôtel Dieu

de la Cité

Hotel de Ville

P.Louis Phillipe

Bras Marie

P.Marie

Ile St Louis

Bras St Louis

P.Sully

P. de la Tournelle

Faculté des Sciences

Place de la Bastille

Port de Plaisance de Paris Arsenal

Canal St Martin

9 Bastille Lock

P.d'Austerlitz

Gare d'Austerlitz

P.de Bercy

Bras de la Monnaie: One way traffic upstream
Bras Marie: One way traffic downstream

Alternating traffic signal
between P. Sully and P. au Change

carousing from trip boats and the near-ceaseless wash of the river traffic.

But just to observe the stretches while cruising to the Arsenal, you cannot fail to be impressed by the abundance of visual glories: the bridges, the sculptures, and the architecture are a constant joy. Two perspectives, especially when viewed from the river, are of the Eiffel Tower and the dramatically contrasting glass mountain of TF1, HQ of French TV. What price the Murdoch's Mammon? ... and yet I say unto you, that even Rupert in all his glory was not arrayed like one of these.

However, just upstream, there is the greater island glory of Notre Dame. It is best viewed from fore and aft; from beam on it is difficult to get far enough away from the towering edifice to be able to experience it whole. There is a one-way system round the island. It affords no inconvenience going upstream – you just keep to the right and carry on – but the downstream route is controlled by traffic lights when descending. After Notre Dame, the entrance to the Port de Plaisance de Paris Arsenal comes as something of a disillusionment. However, the approach will no doubt be completely tidied and improved when the massive works for the new Metro line going on nearby/above/underneath are completed.

Although the most expensive berthing facility in Paris, the Port de Plaisance de Paris Arsenal, with its relative peace and quiet, and superb location by the Place de la Bastille, has to be the prime candidate for anyone proposing to stay for more than a quick stopover. You can call up on VHF or wait until you arrive and then announce yourself from the listening post on the river pontoon. No matter how good your French, you will probably be welcomed in English. We shall return to the subject of the 'Bastille' Port de Plaisance after the round tour of the inner canals.

PARIS

Towards the end of the 18th century and the Revolution, Paris had two Seines: the Royal and the Vulgar. It also used to require an exceedingly tricky feat of navigation. Many of us wax eloquent about the charms of Paris, but sailors were heard to call it Misery Valley, because of all the hauling against foul tides ... by men with ropes round their necks.

Perhaps the best way of becoming acquainted with Paris is by taking a trip on one of the (in?)famous Bateaux Mouches. These amazing trip boats with their light'n'-sound and wash after wash can be guaranteed to churn out the history at a real rate of knots. By tradition, the boats have been understood by Brits to be so called because they are like flies, water-boatmen or mosquitoes. In fact, their name allegedly comes from that part of Lyon known as Mouche, where the first proper-prop trip boats were built for the Paris Exhibition in 1867.

THE CANAL ROUTE TO THE BASTILLE

The inner-city canals, the St-Denis, the St-Martin and the Ourcq, are hardly ever frequented by visitors. However, the few hundred metres of the St-Martin canal are well and truly known, since they are now the Paris Arsenal marina itself, leading, via Lock No. 9, 'La Bastille', straight into the river, and thus known as 'The Gateway to the Seine'.

The three canals offer more than just an offhand change from the regular route up the Seine from PK 33 to the Port de Plaisance de Paris Arsenal just past PK 0. There is some fuel economy, the total canal distance being no more than 12km, but there is no saving of hours – any husbandry with fuel must be offset by the time spent negotiating the 16 locks, filling in forms, and generally talking to lock-keepers and passers-by ... all of whom want to know from whence you came, and all of whom feel they deserve to be kept happy and have their questions answered. Moreover, there is the intriguing but potentially time-consuming exploration of the fascinating soft underbelly of Paris, with its hard-cast-iron bridges; perhaps musing on the thought that

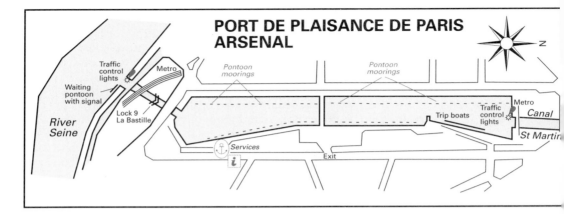

if it were not for the all-pervasive and quite puissant presence of the arch police-voyeur Maigret, one might indeed meet with those of Toulouse-Lautrec or Genet, those archetypal artists of *les bas-fonds*: the depths of back-street life. Ghostly forms in their likeness, if not their garb, still inhabit the shadows.

In general, these inner navigable waterways are open to leisure craft without charge, as are the locks and the lifting bridges on L'Ourcq. There is a special toll for locking through the canals St Denis and St Martin. Mooring is free for the first seven days on the canal and canalised river Ourcq outside Paris; so is the first day within Paris, and some of these inner-city moorings have water and electricity laid on at good mooring spots. Even when charges are levied, they must be reckoned as naught when compared with the fees levied by the Port de Plaisance de Paris Arsenal. In 1996, the toll there began even for modest craft at c.£17 per day. We will look at these canals in the order St-Denis, St-Martin and L'Ourcq.

CANAL ST DENIS

After the junction with the Ile de St-Denis, you continue for 4km until the dark arches of the double lock appear on a bend on the port hand. They present a gloomy, even dismal, prospect from the Seine, but fortunately there is a new waiting pontoon in good and sturdy order from which you can signal the lock-keeper. Once you have locked through, all is sweetness and light as you look up again to a sky that can suddenly seem much closer.

The Canal St Denis extends 6·6km from the Seine at St Denis to the Canal de l'Ourcq and its famous Bassin de la Villette. There are seven paired locks in the 4·5km-long canal, which rises a total of 24m. The large chamber is 62·25m long and 8·1m wide, while the small chamber measures 38·9 by 5·2m. The maximum draught throughout is 2·6m, and the bridges have a minimum headroom of 4·6m. With the exception of Porte de Paris and St-Denis (Nos 5 and 6, under remote control from La Briche, No. 7) all the locks are manned. Normally they are open every day between 0630 and 1915. Nos 1, 5, 6 and 7 can be called from their posts or on VHF.

The Canal St-Denis runs from the Seine to the Canal de l'Ourcq and the Bassin de la Villette. It is the busiest of the three canals in Paris, passing through predominantly industrial suburbs, with numerous private quays used by commercial barges. The St-Denis canal is the workhorse waterway of these Paris canals. While affording little in the way of scenic displays, it does offer the kind of speedy passage that is not to be found when negotiating the Bassin de la Villette and the Canal St-Martin, but if all you want is access to L'Ourcq it is better to use the Canal St Martin, via the Bastille lock and the Paris Arsenal marina.

It takes about half an hour to sort out the fees and admin with the helpful lock staff. You then move into the system where the next two are remotely controlled from St

Denis. It takes another 30 minutes to negotiate these and arrive at the first attended lock, which has no floating bollard (an unhappy surprise this). It is an easy passage all the way to the last lock, Du Pont de Flandre, which is a vast edifice – much in need of serious restoration, but with only minimal work apparently under way. More paperwork is required here, and in the end it takes two to two and a half hours before you pass into the next section, with a T-junction that has the Canal de l'Ourcq to port and the Bassin de la Villette to starboard. The Canal de l'Ourcq leads us away from the centre of Paris, so before following its tempting trail we will pursue the Canal St-Martin.

CANAL ST MARTIN

The Canal St-Martin runs from the Bassin de la Villette to the Seine. There is a lifting bridge on the St-Martin/L'Ourcq side of La Villette. It is in operation all day every day and is automatic. Near the Bassin bridges, there are mooring bollards for boats going upstream on the right bank and for boats going downstream on the left.

The nine locks are 42m by 7·8m, with an authorised draught of 1·9m, and the fixed bridges offer 4·37m headroom. Normally they are open every day between 0800 and 2315. There are two swing bridges and eight double staircase locks, all of which are manned and controlled by lights. Four and a half kilometres long, the Canal St-Martin consists of alternating wide-open-sky *biefs* and tunnels that run under many boulevards. During the day, pools of light shine through the ventilation holes, adding extra shafts of magic as you pass through the otherwise dark tunnels. The locks attract hundreds of tourists, most poised ready to stand and stare ... and shoot – with cameras, of course. The last part of the canal, the tunnel into Paris Arsenal, runs right underneath the Place de la Bastille. The actual obelisk inaugurated by Louis-Philippe stands directly above the canal, so that when the revolutionaries started to burn down the hated monuments all they had to do was set fire to a barge loaded with paraffin: flames arose, roared and reached, but just like Joan of Arc's innards, the bronze did not melt. Unlike her heart, however, the pile still stands.

In the Bassin de la Villette, all and sundry delight in telling visitors where to go and not to go – and even where to get off and how long they will have to wait. This is done with great relish and gusto by the commercial trip-boat operators, who will delight in spelling out a wait of hours, since their own comings and goings take absolute priority ... in mooring as well as locking. According to them, it can take hours for your 'leisure crafts' turn to come after all the trip boats.

Gallic exaggeration, I think not: for example, in spite of calling the Villette lock-keeper first at about 1300 and speaking to him three times on VHF (each time being told to wait just a few minutes), it was not until 1700 that I was allowed to pass through – in splendid isolation. Locking through the four doubles and the long Arsenal tunnel took another hour and a half (including more paperwork), and it was not until 1900 that I was securely berthed in the Port de Plaisance de Paris Arsenal.

And that word 'securely' prompts a crooked smile: in spite of the presence of the two black-jacketed guards, each armed and accompanied by a large Alsatian dog, *Valcon* was broken into during the early hours of the morning. I had gone to sleep about midnight and got up about five, having heard nothing untoward during the night. Some person or persons unknown had opened the door, got on board, and unearthed my handbag from its hiding place. I found it slashed: wallets and credit cards had gone, but the money purse with more than £20 in coin was still there. Why the bag should have been slashed, looted and left (taking minutes) when it could have gone *in toto* in seconds I never understood. At the *capitainerie* there was much sympathy but not a lot of real concern; during the day I discovered that there had been two more robberies that night and that only a few nights before, an elderly lady had been mugged.

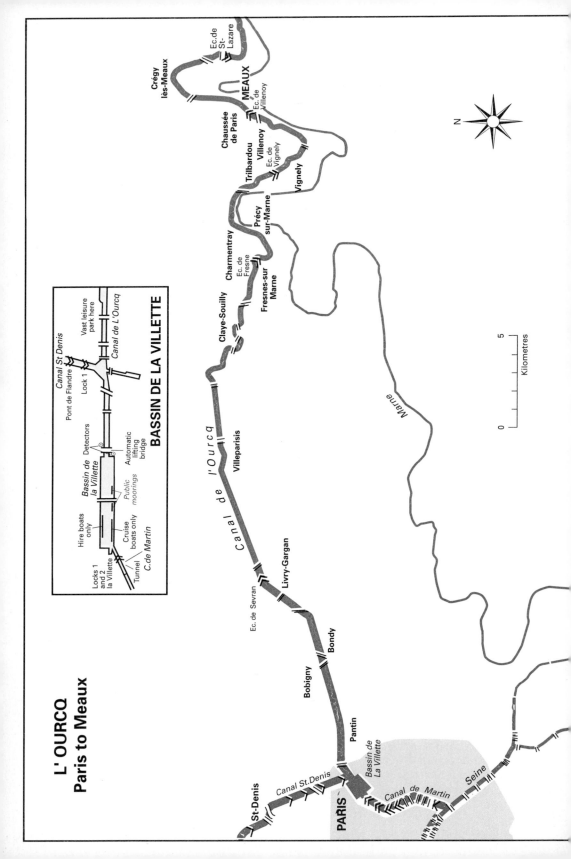

Above Amfreville: the first and the last; where the locks separate the tidal from the non-tidal waters of the Seine – a river which is never tame; has now been fully tamed; but is just that much tamer upstream of Amfreville

Below The huge and hugely crumbling fortress walls of the Château Gaillard, overpoweringly and overtoweringly dominating the diminutive Ports de Plaisance below

Above Barges still abound at Conflans Ste Honorine; fewer now than in days of yore – but still enough to deny key quay space to all but dinghies and tenders unless you can 'barge' your way in.

Below Suresnes is the last lock before Paris proper (or improper, as you prefer). No one has proffered a definitive meaning or derivation – but the keepers ensure that All is Serene.

Above Like a set for *The Glass Mountain* designed by Sean Kenny, the glazed walls of the HQ of France's most popular TV channel present a façade of shimmer and glitz as it heralds the centre of the capital city.

Below In contrast to the most over-statement of TF1 are the refurbished and garlanded *péniches*. In their retirement, they are tried and tested as homes for the retired and rested.

Above From on high, the spires of Notre Dame aspire to spike the sky eternally...

Below ...while down below, the 'daily round' (the island) is the 'common task' (of the Bâteaux Mouches). No styx here, of course; but plenty of ferrymen

Above Once, the dread word Bastille meant a fate worse than death; and its companion, the Arsenal was all Guns and no Roses. Now, the Arsenal is the prime Port de Plaisance and the Bastille has an entirely different lock – but still offers a fate worse than ...?

Below Just above Paris, both banks of the Seine are rose to riparians whose imposingly beautiful mansions (châteaux even) proudly proclaim their past and present positions: historically, culturally, socially...and, of course, financially

Above The approach to Melun Backwater Halte de Plaisance is almost obscured by overhanging trees as it poses crumbling quays and the occasional wreck. These two craft are among the more attractive

Below Valcon: if not quite in splendid isolation, certainly alone and visited only by swans. The prettily decked road bridge and the town centre are merely minutes away. This is no place to comment 'Hard Cheese', being the centre of the very best soft Brie.

Above St Mammès: All change! To port is the
Petite Seine and to starboard the Canal du Loing:
the watery way to the Med

Below Some of the bridges on the Oise are framed
by backcloths that are quite atypical of this
generally scenic river.....

.....as is happily shown by this rear idyllic sketch.

Below Compiègne is not head of navigation of the Oise; but it is head and shoulders above any other location on the river. Here, we look out from the modest and warmly welcoming marina through the small entrance on a typical view.

I reported to the Commissariat de Voie Publique du 4ᵉᵐᵉ Arrondissement, where 'Oui Mon Capitaine' resounded so frequently that it seemed possible at one time that Maigret himself was lurking here. The Capitaine's verdict was: Thugs for Drugs!

The canal has a certain Parisian charm, with its elegant iron footbridges, and it has been a tourist attraction for several years, with a regular trip-boat service along the canal. In the heart of the city, with inexpensive quayside moorings, some with water and electricity, it is a boater's delight.

The 1,600m tunnel at the Arsenal end has a one-way traffic system controlled by lights. Stopping is prohibited, and boats of more than 20m LOA cannot turn. The marina is a delight for the trip-boat sightseers, who enjoy observing the antics of those moored in the Paris Arsenal basin.

Alternatively, you can approach the canal from the Seine. There is a waiting pontoon outside the lock in the river and another inside by the *capitainerie*. Both have calling posts, so you can wait without inconvenience whichever way you are going. Call the harbourmaster as instructed, or on VHF Ch 9. The lock, No. 9, La Bastille, the only single lock on the Canal St-Martin, will then be prepared for you. Remotely controlled by the *capitainerie* at the Port de Plaisance, it forms the well used gateway to the Seine.

In spite of any wait, the entry into Paris Arsenal marina must always afford at least a small thrill: you can moor within metres of the Place de la Bastille, its splendidly controversial opera centre, and, of course, some of the finest eating places in the world.

THE CANAL DE L'OURCQ AND THE BASSIN DE LA VILLETTE

The canalised river Ourcq is different from the Canal St-Denis and the Canal St-Martin in that it is not really a city-centre canal at all; more a deviation into Paris's outlying rural regions. The canal provides the water-pound supplies for operating the locks of the St-Denis and St-Martin canals in Paris. It also provides water for factories in Paris. The navigable waterway is 110km, made up of three sections: the canalised river (10km with four locks) which runs from the current head of navigation at Port aux Pêches downstream to Mareuil-sur-Ourcq; the canal itself (90km with four locks) from Mareuil to Les Pavillons-sous-Bois, where it is 1·5m deep and 11m wide; and the last, 'open', stretch into what is sometimes facetiously called the 'canal roundabout' at La Villette.

The river Ourcq rises in the forest of Villers Cotterets, up in the Aisne, and after La Ferté Milon (almost at the present head of navigation) it descends into breezy, cheesy Brie country. The river used to flow directly into the Marne at Mary-sur-Marne. A canalisation programme was started in 1529, but not put into operation until 1636. It was very much a modest scheme until Napoleon Bonaparte put his stamp on it. He radically changed it all in 1802 by decreeing a canal with aqueduct to be constructed to reach right into the heart of La Villette basin. Under the Master, it was all done and dusted in seven years, and just under 20 years afterwards it was fully functional right up to Mareuil-sur-Ourcq (only 10km from the present head of navigation), with serious commercial shipping moving between Meaux and Paris. Improvements and additions were made in the 1920s and it has remained the same ever since, but all commercial craft ceased using it in the 1960s.

Sevran, its first lock, is manned and permits passage between 0900 and 1700. After this all the Ourcq locks are self-service, for which a key 'A' is necessary. The Congis bridge is worked the same way, but skippers of craft of more than 2m air draught must contact the navigation service in advance at ☎ 01 60 09 53 90. They will come out to meet you. A key may be obtained from the lock-keeper at Sevran or the *capitainerie* at Paris Arsenal. You can also get the well designed brochure of the waterway published by the Mairie de Paris. It describes in detail the working of the keys, locks and

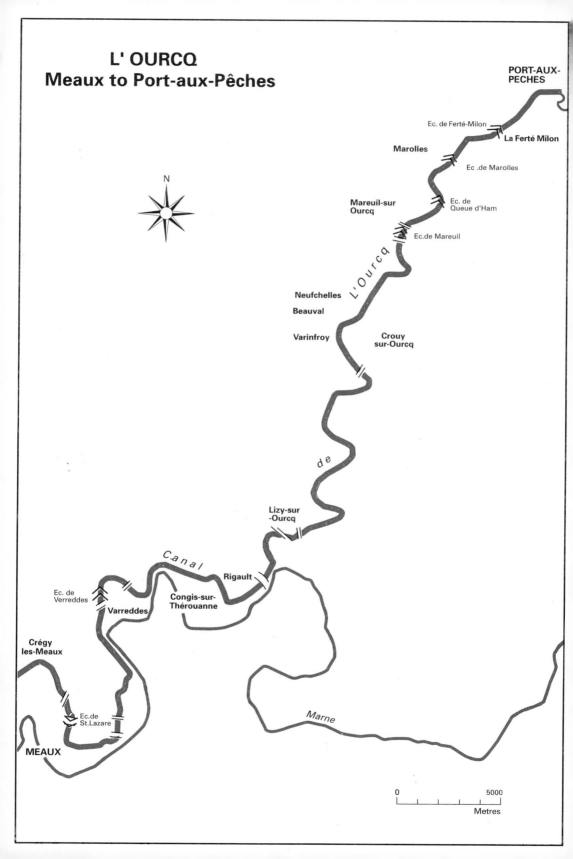

bridges, and contains some hilarious sketches. It is called *Le réseau fluvial de la Ville de Paris: Guide du plaisancier.*

The six locks in the 97km canal section (Sevran No. 1 to Varreddes No. 6) are standard single gates, while the four locks in the 11km of the canalised river section have double gates, sloping sides and floating pontoons. The permitted depth in the first, 'Grande' section of the canal is 2·6m. After Sevran the 'Petite' section is technically limited to 0·8m, but craft up to 1·1m are permitted at owners' risk – and commanded strictly to adhere to the centre of the *bief*.

The environs of the first reaches of the Canal de l'Ourcq are given over to commerce and industry, but it does not take long before it becomes a non-urban experience. Its 110km soon leave behind the urban/suburban for what feels like the heart of the countryside and the companionship of the river Marne. Fuelling points are few, and it would be wise to bunker up tanks and spares before setting off – otherwise long walks will be the order of the day. It is for those who care not for la dolce vita, speed and prying eyes –being suited specially for those with life/time to stand and stare.

By the time Pavillons-sous-Bois has been reached, after Pantin, Romainville and Bobigny, the canal narrows and is only navigable by smaller boats. Sevran lock and those which follow are all only 3·7m wide, with the section between Vignely and Varreddes cutting that down to 3·1m. The usual VNF-type 'promises' have been issued to the effect that works are in the pipeline (if not the canal) to improve the waterway and its facilities, and also to widen the locks and better the restrictive heights of bridges.

At Sevran, the lock-keeper almost ceremoniously hands over the key without which you can make no progress. He will also arrange to meet you at the lift bridge at Claye Souilly, if needed. As mentioned above, the bridge has a restricting height of 2m air draught, and if you are under the limit you can just cruise through. I always think it is a good idea to have him on hand, just in case ... and he doesn't seem to mind – quite likes it, in fact.

Trilbardou, at PK 38, is worth a proper stop. Here you can see one of the two pumping stations of which the city fathers are so proud. These are feats of precise engineering that pump water from the Marne to feed the canal; the Villiers Les Rigault station is the other. The huge paddle wheel at Trilbardou station was designed and built by the famous hydraulic engineer Alphonse Sagebien. It is an amazing construction. 11m in diameter and 6m wide, it has 70 wooden blades worked by a set of four pumps that discharge approximately 27,000m^3 per day. The water is lifted to a height of 12m, the difference in level between the Marne and the Ourcq canal when it was dug out of the hillside here. It was completed in 1869 and has been kept in perfect working condition ever since. In the village are a *château* and a church, both worth a visit.

Next come Vignely and Villenoy, at PK 40 and PK 47: the first of the DIY locks. You start with the key you first thought of, and then move on key by key, stage by stage until you have done. The key you end up with is the one you take to the next lock to start all over again. This system of working with keys could easily have been devised and described by Lewis Carroll (the mad engineering mathematical Charles Dodgson), first because the whole idea could have leapt fully armed from *Alice in Wonderland*, and second because of the earnest injunction, 'Begin at the beginning', the King said, gravely, 'and go on till you come to the end: then stop.'

Cheese lovers will want to know that, while you cannot get to Melun for the strong Brie that is made there, it is possible to get to Meaux, the Ourcq offering a back-door alternative to the Marne.

MEAUX

Meaux was once a champagne town, and now it is a tourist centre – but still with its roots in agriculture – betokened by the eponymous cheese which starts life in the famous dairy pastures of Brie.

The cathedral of St Stephen was created through the 12th and 16th centuries. The flamboyant façade and the darkly shingled Black Tower are famous. While the limestone exterior is in very poor condition, inside the cathedral all is lightness and sightliness. Part of the nave dates back to the 13th century, and the 14th-century transepts are gorgeous, brilliantly Gothic. Meaux had a famous bishop, one Jacques Bossuet, later to be known as the 'Eagle of Meaux' because of his Spartan ways and Draconian discipline. The ambulatory leads you to the black marble that marks his tomb. In season, there is a son et lumière in the Episcopal Precinct.

Between Meaux and the head of navigation, there are many places where it is relaxing to stop and pleasing to investigate. Varreddes and Congis-sur-Therouanne, both upstream from Meaux, 15km and 20km respectively, have open, laid-out park and leisure areas. The *château*, reservoir and ponds are good for a full day's exploration in fine weather. After another 5km comes Lizy-sur-Ourcq, a legendary sepulchral site for nomadic bohemians and other eccentrics, including circus folk. There are enough catacombs to justify twinning the place with Tombstone, Arizona. The much used and abused castle and its towers are nearby.

After 13km and five more bridges, near the village of Crouy-sur-Ourcq, the ruins of the eponymous castle and that of Gesvres are worth visiting; only 3km further on are more historic delights in the village of Neufchelles, especially the church, the *château* and the priory. There is also the nearby Commandery of the Knights Templar at Moisy, up the offshoot Clignon canal. By the time we reach La Ferté Milon, after 10km, we are close to the head of the navigation. There should be a notable fortress here, as decreed by the Duc d'Orléans. However, both he and his grandiose plans were Put to the Claymore, as it were, at the hands of John the Fearless of Burgundy. The walls are impressive, but more to be appreciated are the works of Racine, who was born here. The restored house now functions as the writer's museum.

The end of the navigation comes with the low-key experience of Port aux Pêches, where the non-navigable reaches of the Ourcq continue to starboard. There is not a tremendous amount of room for manoeuvring, but the posts and quays clearly indicate the mooring places. So, after 100km of quite miniature waterway, it is time to return to the mother river where we left her, in Paris.

La Haute Seine – Paris to Montereau

The Haute Seine starts virtually from the Port de Plaisance de Paris Arsenal marina. Just across the river you will see the river police boats. Their crews usually seem to be enjoying a thoroughly relaxed lifestyle, but in a flash they can be alongside, ready to check fuel tanks for the famous 'red' diesel (*le rouge* is illegal in leisure craft). After less than 5km en route to the Mediterranean comes the junction with the Marne, which goes more or less straight ahead at Charenton/Alfortville. For the Seine, you take the starboard fork, leaving to port what must be a contender for the prize of The Biggest Chinese Restaurant in the World.

The first of the 19 locks on the Seine upstream of Paris is Port à l'Anglais, at PK 161. It is just as large as the big ones on the lower Seine and is just as smoothly worked. There are two locks, and you need to await the keeper's instructions to know whether to use the one on the left bank or the one on the right. You may experience a wait here, as some of the keepers can be very keen on their paperwork. While not quite unconscionably dragging out the law's delay, nor piling on the full agony of the insolence of office, they can delay your progress more than somewhat by demanding everything: ships' papers, log, radio licence, insurance certificate, and also the obligatory VNF licence, known as a *vignette*, and often referred to as *papiers* or *cartes* – but most frequently signalled by the lock-keeper drawing a rectangle in the air with one or both hands. Such is the whimsy behind the controllers of the system that you may equally pass through without let or hindrance.

The first boatyard is to be found on the right bank at Choisy-le-Roi (PK 158). It maintains a long string of mooring buoys well out in the river, and while they do not impress with bright paint or outward signs of servicing, they look satisfactorily strong. The boatyard's setting is neither comely nor appealing. The police seem to be in attendance at very regular intervals, and that can be interpreted for good or ill. Nevertheless, it offers a useful emergency service, and shoresides there are town facilities not far away.

The next possible stop comes on the right bank just before Villeneuve-St-George (PK 154), where there is a so-called Port de Plaisance. The place is mainly a yacht club, with two preoccupations: their pretentious presentation of a self-satisfied image, and an obsession with the fast lane in all its connotations. They have neither the time, the space, the propensity nor the courtesy to welcome visitors. The small space immediately next the marina set aside for public use is not only of suspect depth, but it also has rusted mooring posts with dangerous overhead wires that deny access to all craft with more than 2·5m air draught. There are few facilities directly to hand. Although the possibility of a free mooring is always an attraction (indeed, for some canal users it is an imperative over all other considerations), on this occasion, and on balance, it must surely be better to move on.

The first choice comes with the very new and up-to-date Port Premier, at PK 148. Ablon lock intervenes after a couple of kilometres, but after only one kilometre more the marina will appear on the right bank immediately after the railway bridge. In fact, it will not appear, for it is well tucked away, almost hidden among the trees that are a feature of its rural setting. It is a private marina and rapidly becoming a residential development: not quite in the Solent Swish league, but smart and sophisticated nonetheless. While there is little room to accommodate visitors, most berths being in constant occupation by the owners, many of whom have fled Paris, visitors are made extremely welcome, and the marina facilities themselves are superb. Although not inexpensive, it has a lot to offer and is increasing its facilities month by month. Some shops are no more than a brisk walk away; the township of Vigneux-sur-Seine is a goodly distance, but worth the effort. If you are allocated a berth near the river, you will soon discover to your discomfort that you are also near the main railway line – and the traffic runs through the night. It is essential to reserve a place well ahead of your visit. They take phone bookings (☎ 01 69 03 57 60).

Only 2km after Port Premier is the Port aux Cerises marina, at PK 146 near Draveil. It is part of a major leisure/pleasure holiday centre, and not primarily run as a boating facility. However, the pontoons are sound, depth is good, and the all-night security is first rate. On the ungood front, there are very few water taps, no mains electricity, and the toilets must be considered 'basic' at best. Somewhat unexpectedly, by the visitors' moorings there is a live theatre in a barge.

It is important to arrive early in the afternoon – certainly not after 1600, since the office staff tend towards eccentric hours. You will pay your fee and be issued with a security key. Otherwise, while you may get a free mooring, you will be berth-bound within the compound for the night, unless you unship the dinghy and brave the security guard. Many skippers complain at the fixed prices set at Port aux Cerises (in 1996 reductions had actually been made; the charges were: up to 7m FF40; over 7m FF80). There are plenty of good shops on both sides of the river, but those at Draveil are the nearest. There is a charismatic bar just by the crossroads, and nearby a non-charismatic but very large and expensive Chinese restaurant. The prices of the first are chalked on a board, while those of the second are out of sight.

There are moorings at the Club Nautique at Le Port aux Malades (PK 144), but

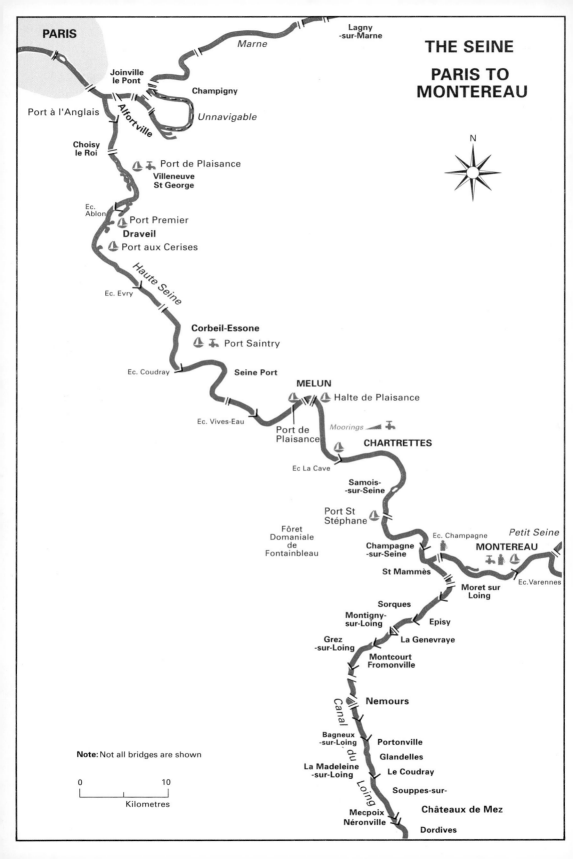

the facility is so small and full that it is not a candidate. So it is on to PK 142, where just upstream of the Pont de Ris Orangis there is the Vert Logis restaurant. It is a superb place (sometimes with superb plaice, but always with many other kinds of highly priced fish dishes) where you might just be lucky enough to have the chef in person come out to take your ropes. There is a small public quay just downstream, and the Champrosay Club Nautique is next door upstream, with a membership that is little in evidence.

There are moorings for small craft at Evry Petit Bourg and Corbeil Essones, but in the main they are occupied by sailing boats, dinghies and canoes – modest craft even at their largest. They are also much used by ski enthusiasts. The same applies to the well advertised Port Saintry. In practice, it turns out to be of little substance, both metaphorically and literally. Craft of more than 8m LOA must strain its pontoons when attacked by the big wakes of big barges. I judged that *Valcon*, the pontoons and I would not survive undamaged through the night.

Actually, the next best halt is the Coudray lock (No. 7: PK 130). This is a large establishment, and while the sluices are well controlled, it can still be a lively experience, requiring constant attention to rope work. Nearby there is a spacious wall with wooded verges and the most comely Auberge de Barrage on the north bank. Sadly, it has no safe direct access for boats.

Before the next main feature, Melun (PK 110), there are some modest stopping places. Most are sailing clubs with very small pontoons (for example, the Centre Nautique Maurice Dunand at PK 125), but two are out of the general run. The first is by the old lock de la Citanguette, where there is a small quay for the hotel, but where the rest of the moorings are taken up (apparently permanently) by barges. After Vives Eaux (well named, for it is just as lively as Coudray), lock No. 4, the second is a small Port de Plaisance just outside Melun at PK 112. It is essentially a mini-marina, although it does house larger craft in spite of its narrow entrance. Its riverside stone quay has a very good depth.

To reach the Halte Nautique at Melun, you leave the main navigation and proceed to port past a motley collection of boats on the starboard hand. The pontoon comes shortly after, also on the starboard hand, with five white mooring buoys to port. None of it is in best repair, but it affords convenient access to the town, which is a gem of a place. This is a must of a stopover for enthusiasts of French cheeses, since Brie de Melun is among the best – certainly the most singular of Bries, with a strong salt bite and a mighty aftertaste. The sins of omission at the Halte are completely offset by the general charm of the town and the ample facilities that are close to hand. I have spent many happy days at the pontoon, incredulous that not one other boat appeared wanting to moor. The explanation must be that the quays on the main arm appear to be for mooring, and are always full, while the Halte is hidden away, only showing itself after close investigation.

Although the Halte de Melun branch rejoins the main line further upstream, it is unnavigable for leisure craft. You may, however, see soldiers and marines moving through the water pretty speedily in substantial craft, but they are on manoeuvres and have rights over the area. Lesser mortals must retreat to the downstream junction before continuing upstream. After the last bridge out of Melun (the one that is wondrously named Pet au Diable – the translation of which I do not believe) it is no distance at all to another splendid stopping place: the Port de Plaisance de Chartrettes.

This small bankside 'marina' facility appears on the port hand just after La Cave lock, No. 3. The moorings are best taken bows to, since the good depths run out as weed takes over close to the bank. The establishment is run from the barge at the downstream end, where you will be welcomed by a variety of animal/bird life, including a friendly goose. Mains water and electricity work well and the first night's mooring is free. This is a quiet spot, with a restaurant close by and a supermarket twenty minutes' walk away. There are only two potential drawbacks: there is no tele-

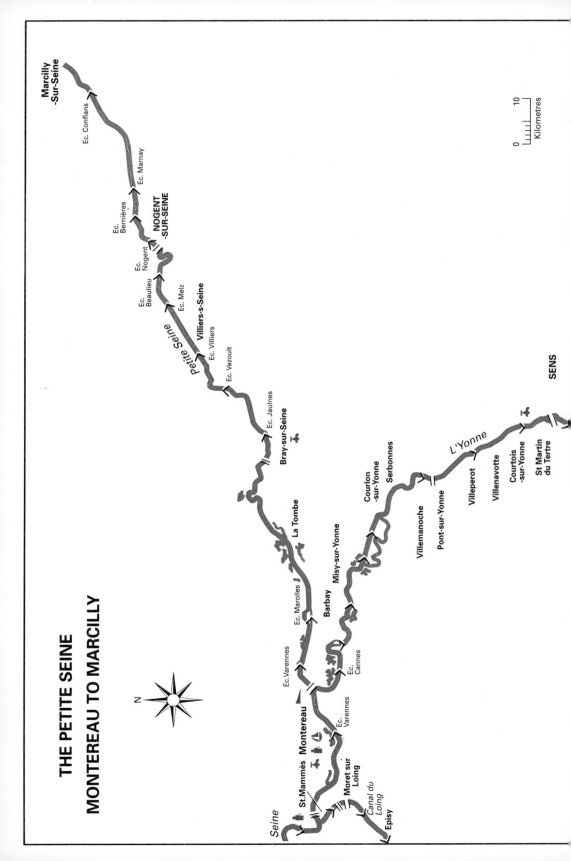

THE PETITE SEINE
MONTEREAU TO MARCILLY

N

Seine

Marcilly
-Sur-Seine

Ec. Conflans

Ec. Marnay

Ec.
Bernières

**NOGENT
-SUR-SEINE**

Ec.
Nogent

Ec.
Beaulieu

Ec. Melz

Villiers-s-Seine

Petite Seine

Ec. Villiers

Ec. Vezoult

Ec. Jaulnes

Bray-sur-Seine

La Tombe

Ec. Marolles

Barbay

Misy-sur-Yonne

**Courlon
-sur-Yonne**

Serbonnes

Ec.Varennes

Ec.
Varennes

Ec. Cannes

Villemanoche

Pont-sur-Yonne

Villeperot

L'Yonne

Villenavotte

**Courtois
-sur-Yonne**

**St Martin
du Tertre**

SENS

St.Mammès **Montereau**

**Moret sur
Loing**

*Canal du
Loing*

Episy

0   10
|__|__|___|___|
Kilometres

phone, and at weekends in the season, activity is hectic at the end of the moorings where the f(r)iends of the Bassin de Vitesse de Bois-le-Roi reign and rave supreme. If this performance is not to your taste, there is a very quiet anchorage a few kilometres upstream not far from the village of Samois-sur-Seine. It is a small loop off the main channel, much used by recuperating barge folk. Red buoys designate it as a definite Slow Boat strait.

A stopover quite different from Chartrettes and Samois is Port de Stéphane Mallarmé, on the left bank at PK 90. The pontoons are all new; some of their advertised facilities are so 'new' that only recently they were not up and running. The last pontoon is set aside for visitors; moor downstream and as near to the bank as you can, as the flow can hinder mooring and the wash can be heavy when the mad skipper of an overloaded early-bird *péniche* sends a visitation with a mighty rock'n'roll effect. The local supermarket is a good (walkable) distance and there are choice restaurants in the vicinity. The biggest temptation is the bar at the nearby crossroads. It is a place of unexpected character, and Saturday is Special Couscous Night – a positive joy of an inexpensive treat. The proprietor is a kind of Che Guevara/Omar Sharif *manqué* who delights in exercising his unique brand of English.

Just over 10km ahead comes the parting of the ways for most Brits, for to starboard is the Canaux du Centre route for the Mediterranean. There is a big fuelling station to port after the junction. It is much used by barges and you may have to wait. Since this is a barge centre, services are available. St-Mammès lies on one side of the river and Champagne-sur-Seine on the other. There is due to be a new marina-style facility on the right bank of the Canal du Loing: planning permission has been given and preparations are in hand – as the usual story goes. On the starboard bank of the Seine there are good moorings with easy access to the town. If these are full, you just move on 1km upstream to the Base Nautique and Sailing Club of St-Mammès.

La Petite Seine – Montereau to Marcilly

We now move into the last reach of the Seine. For some time it has been reining in its girth and its banks have been slowly approaching one another. From now on it becomes increasingly approachable – perhaps, as it were, affable and even friendly. The next major halt, Montereau, is at a junction, as was St-Mammès; this one is with the river Yonne, which takes you to the Bourgogne and Nivernais canals, and then on to the Mediterranean via the Saône and Rhône.

There is a possible stopover at the old Madeleine lock at PK 77, where mooring is free. However, it does have certain drawbacks: the proximity of the Centrale Thermique EDF de Montereau is one, and the fact that it is usually completely taken up with sundry craft in divers states of neglect, if not wreckage, is another. The crunch factor is perhaps that neither the close environment nor its companions seem very salutary. Most folk will want to move on through the next lock, Varennes 1, at PK 71, and after a couple of kilometres moor at the pleasant green sward just to starboard after the bridge and junction at Montereau (PK 68). There is usually a vacant place, and there are plenty of shops nearby. The villagers are all friendly, and more than willing to pass the time of day or night with someone with some gossip to share.

Once the submerged lurking stones, pillars and posts on the right bank of Surville have been left behind, the Seine continues to change its character. Becoming even more 'sequoine', it seems to assuage itself into a calmly picturesque and quite composed character. The effect is noticeable on the lock-keepers also; they become much more concerned with idle, friendly chat than with expediting your progress upstream. The first lock is Marolles No. 13 at PK 61, immediately next its namesake village, Marolles-sur-Seine, just under 7km from Montereau. It is a charming spot, with deep-water moorings to a grassy bank. There are some regular boaters here who will welcome you quietly, help you to moor in the best place they can find, and then leave

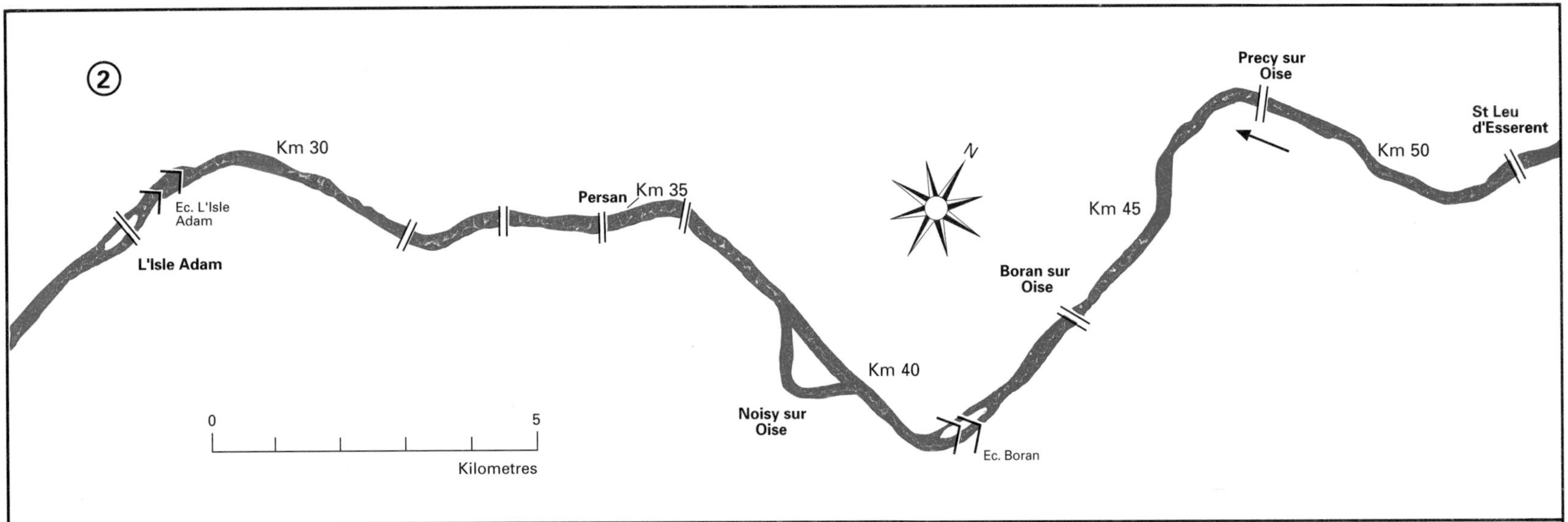
2
Precy sur Oise
St Leu d'Esserent
Km 30
Km 50
Persan
Km 35
Ec. L'Isle Adam
Km 45
L'Isle Adam
Boran sur Oise
Km 40
0
5
Noisy sur Oise
Kilometres
Ec. Boran

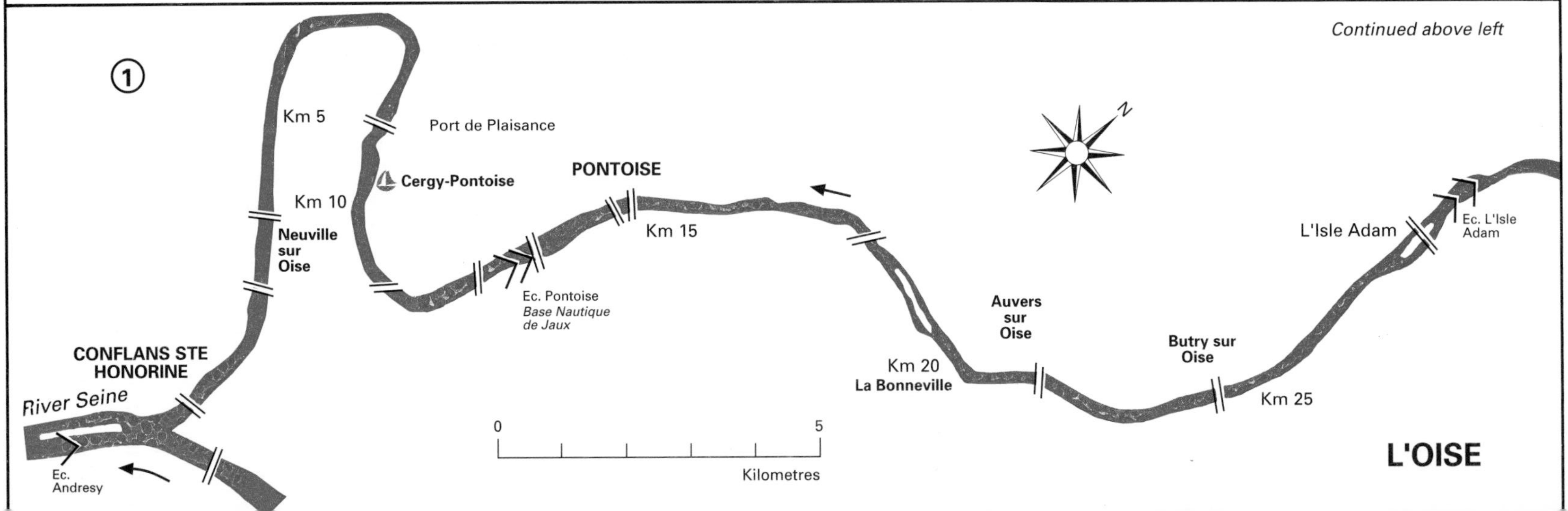
Continued above left
1
Km 5
Port de Plaisance
Cergy-Pontoise
PONTOISE
Km 10
Km 15
L'Isle Adam
Ec. L'Isle Adam
Neuville sur Oise
Ec. Pontoise
Base Nautique de Jaux
Auvers sur Oise
Butry sur Oise
CONFLANS STE HONORINE
Km 20
La Bonneville
Km 25
River Seine
0
5
Ec. Andresy
Kilometres
L'OISE

you, in the friendliest manner possible, to your own devices ... hoping that you will be good enough to do the same for them as and when.

Just downstream there had been plans for a marina, but they failed; just upstream (PK 58) there is supposedly a Port de Plaisance, but all that can be seen in the small 'lake' is a bank encumbered with trees. Here, at La Tombe, the navigation deviates to port, leaving to starboard the now unused, but apparently well kept, canal stretch to Bray-sur-Seine, the next small town, 12km away.

Bray has a double pontoon in good order, pleasantly sited by a park and shaded by trees. It is a delightful spot in a delightful village. All facilities are nearby: traditional shops and bars in the village to the right, and food and DIY supermarkets to the left. There is also a leisure centre and bathing pool. The pontoon is without mains, but if this be the small price one has to pay for the delight of Bray, it is no hardship at all. It is the kind of place where all the people in the small township seem to know one another and are just as ready to get to know you. On one occasion I almost got completely involved in a weekend wedding. The locals said it was 'normale'. The old-fashioned shopping is excellent, and the supermarket provides the rest – especially some more than drinkable plonk at bargain prices.

A couple of kilometres upstream is Jaulnes lock, No. 9. It is to be approached with caution, for the current can exert quite a pull, and to starboard where the weir has its run there is a collection of broken piles that beggars belief. Well in advance of the lock, there are traffic control lights to prevent the only too predictable accident-about-to-happen that is the sum and substance of the place. In dramatic contrast is the next lock, Vezoult, No. 8, where major works have provided a new lock and a new channel. Everything at the lock is now new and modern. Indeed, all has been sweetness and light since the infamous *bajoyers inclinés* were replaced. There is a quiet mooring spot just before the lock gates, with nothing but fields, woods and water to hold your attention – supplies are unavailable in the immediate vicinity.

Supplies are in fact 17km distant at Nogent-sur-Seine, with three locks in between. After Vezoult there is a 10km straight canal stretch, with the unnavigable river to starboard. When the two waterways unite again after Beaulieu, the Seine becomes a really secluded river (with just one short speedboat basin). Nogent appears after 4km of really winding waterway. The town quay is to starboard, with a sign to indicate the depths of water available. Industry and commerce are obvious, but the town itself is an attractive example of a traditional French community rooted in the past, but missing out on nothing that is up to date: offering, indeed, the best of both worlds – unless, that is, you happen to have strong views on nuclear power, in which case the place will not endear itself to you.

And what a pleasant note on which to leave the Seine, for although there are nearly 20km of canal and river to Marcilly, theoretically navigable for craft up to 1·4m (or only 1·2m, depending upon your reference datum), I was advised that these depths were optimistic, and that Nogent is best viewed as the head of the navigation. And what a navigation indeed it is, the Seine, from its confused estuary, bleak outlook and tidal forces at Le Havre, with its limited opportunities for mooring, to this quiet, well behaved stream set in agreeable countryside where mooring represents no problem and most of life's necessities are never far away.

L'Oise – Conflans Ste Honorine to Compiègne

After the large-spread breadths of the Seine, the river Oise offers a more modest feeling – once, that is, the heavy commercial section dominated by Conflans has been left behind. It is actually no more than a couple of kilometres before the country joys of Jouy le Moutier hove into view, soon followed by the prettily laid out and well kept mooring at Vaureal (prohibited to yachts!), and, at PK 9, the Port de Plaisance of Cergy Pontoise.

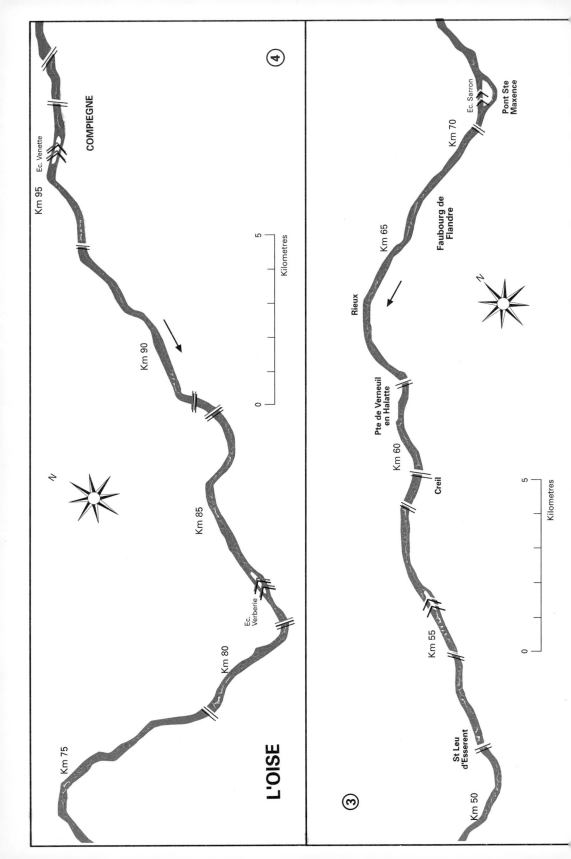

L'OISE

④

COMPIEGNE

Ec. Venette
Km 95

Km 90

Km 85

Ec. Verberie
Km 80

Km 75

Kilometres
0   5

③

Rieux
Km 65

Pte de Verneuil en Halatte
Km 60

Creil

Km 55

St Leu d'Esserent
Km 50

Km 70
Faubourg de Flandre

Ec. Sarron
Pont Ste Maxence

Kilometres
0   5

This new marina, on the right bank, in the clay-brick glaze, stone and glass Mediterranean style, is an overnight alternative to Conflans and Andresy, while for those who left there early in the morning its bread shop and restaurant must be a temptation. It succeeds in being quiet and sophisticated, swish and rural all at once and all together without any feeling of discord or compromise, and it is of course extremely pleasant to look at and to rest in. The marina has clean and new pontoons, each provided with full facilities, and the staff are friendly and helpful. Inside the new development (a mini Port Solent, with berths going with apartments) everything is contemporary. Electric heating on board is accepted without extra charge while the boat is in use. Half of the development consists of private berths with apartments, while the other half, 110 berths, is open to the public. All modern sanitary, social and leisure facilities are immediately to hand, while a few minutes' walk away the old village offers all the charm, goods and chattels that one expects of a rural riverside community. In spite of some modernisation by people who want a country residence but are not in the Maisons Lafitte bracket, the community is still basically a working agricultural one, offering fresh local groceries and vegetables.

Just over 1km before the first lock on the river, Pontoise, No. 7, on the left bank is the Base Nautique de Jaux. It has first-rate pontoons with good depth and basic services. The welcome is warm and friendly, and the Halte leaves nothing to be desired. Just after the lock, the twinned towns of Pontoise and St-Ouen-l'Aumône offer a sound pontoon and good shopping facilities – but also a goodly measure of town and autoroute traffic. So for sylvan peace one moves on another 5km to a quiet wooded backwater at PK 20, near the village of La Bonneville. There is little but tamed wildlife, and very appealing it is. Shortly after, also quietly found, are the modest pontoons at Auvers and Butry, both extremely pleasant spots.

Next comes the lock and very singular community of L'Isle Adam. There are a few pontoons on the banks well before it, but they are all very small. L'Isle Adam is a veritable shrine to good food, wine, and hedonism writ large. The district has been laid out with some flair to entice the Epicurean good, the self-indulgent bad and the sybaritic rich from near and far to spend, spend, spend. There are pontoon places and buoys for no more than six boats. The banks also afford secure mooring for craft of no more than 1m draught. The mooring (with restaurants) is to starboard just before the bridge and the lock.

ISLE ADAM

While the pontoon at L'Isle Adam is a miniature affair, this is France's largest inland beach; now a popular water-sports centre, it features numerous facilities for yachting, sailing, rowing and canoeing. It is still the centre for pleasure-trip boats that it has been for decades.

Adam de Villiers was given the Oise island castle by Capet's son Robert II (the Pious) in 1014. In the 1500s it went to Constable Anne de Montmorency, and later Louis XIII offered it to the Bourbon Henri II, Prince de Condé. In 1646 Armand de Bourbon, Prince de Conti, moved in with his lavish court. In the 19th century Honoré de Balzac was a regular visitor, and some of his works were set in the area; at the same time Villiers de l'Isle Adam, almost as famous, was busily occupied writing his *Contes cruels*.

While the old *château* of the Conti Princes was destroyed in the Revolution, the old stone bridges, from which good views can be seen, still command admiration, especially the very well known 16th-century Cabouillet bridge. St Martin's 16th-century church, with its complex vaulting, has a 19th-century tower after Trinity church in Paris. The German pulpit and the Bourbon funeral chapel are dramatic. The Cassan pagoda, a truly bizarre technicolour pavilion, rises from a lake, perched on a stone base with arches. Above are wooden pillars (with hidden lighting domes) and the whole is topped with ringlets of bells in bronze. L'Isle Adam forest was maintained for years as a hunting/shooting/killing ground for the Princes de Conti. It consists mainly of oaks, with elms, birches, chestnuts and limes.

If a more economical stop is preferred, there is a well laid Halte on the Persan side of the river opposite Beaumont-sur-Oise. There is a very large Leclerc superstore nearby, and only metres away is the small bar/café 'Chez Nicole'. Both offer a good choice, but Nicole, the lady with the bar, a person of curious character, gives extraordinary value. From Beaumont to Nogent is 24km, with two locks, but there are plenty of modest places to moor en route. At PK 49, on the left bank, the Toutevois hotel has its own pontoon. Navigationally, this is the only tricky stretch: on the bend there are some of the very few buoys to be found on the river. These red buoys mark a shoal area that extends well out towards the left bank. They are not particularly obvious – certainly from downstream.

Nogent-sur-Oise is on the port hand opposite the larger town of Creil. For once there is a good choice of quay moorings, and the two commerce-based towns have plenty of facilities. Just before the next lock, at Sarron (10km on), are the two small communities of Faubourg de Flandre and Pont Ste-Maxence. It is possible to moor after the bridge to starboard, where the depth is good. A certain dexterity will probably be required to rope up, and an equally certain agility required to scale the steeply sloping banks. There are some steps that reach all the way to the street.

It is not absolutely easy to get the boat next them, and without them the ascent can be tricky and sloppy. But please do not be put off: Maxence is a joy and well worth a stopover. It is now about 25km and three locks to Compiègne. There is a stream running at between half and a full knot against you, but the speedy efficiency of the double lock-keepers on this stretch makes up for any small delay the stream may cause. The next lock is Verberie, a pretty and well cared for place; the nearby village of Port Salut is unfortunately not the home of the famous cheese. There is a small pontoon and mooring wall in an attractive setting.

Compiègne is a must, and worth the long wait you may have at the last lock, Venette No. 1, where continuing preference is given to commercial craft, no matter how illogical this sometimes is. The Yacht Club marina base is welcoming, with all services, and hardly demanding when it comes to mooring fees. It is unexpected but reassuring to discover that its president is the head of the local police force. There are good eating places and shops nearby, in particular an inexpensive Routiers restaurant to the left outside the gates and a splendid Moroccan indoor market towards the town on the left. On the river near lock No. 1 there is a first-rate chandler – one of the best I have found in France.

After this the next, and last, place of rest on the river is Janville, just 5km above Compiègne, where the navigable reaches end, and the river joins the Canal Latéral à l'Oise. Janville has for a long time been an important barge centre, and even in these degenerate days it is still busy with barges, the double locks working almost nonstop. However, there is usually a vacant spot on the north side of the locks for a modest yacht to creep into. There is also a vast barge park to the south of the locks, and a small quay just before the one-way system round the island. This is a welcoming community, with a very good basic selection of shops. Most of them are run by one single soul, usually eccentric, peculiar or idiosyncratic – but in the nicest possible way. There is a very good hardware shop fronting the canal, run by a most obliging lady. I have found Janville to be such a welcoming and magnetic place that I cannot say a word against it.

But to end this saga, I must beg your brief indulgence and return to Compiègne. It is an appealing town, although very expensive in the town centre, with an equally appealing marina – and both generous to a fault when it comes to making visitors feel welcome. Compiègne is an absolutely ideal spot, a delight of a place; and it brings to a happy conclusion what I rate as a really memorable experience: the Seine/Oise Odyssey.

General

FRENCH INLAND WATERWAYS REQUIREMENTS

For skippers of boats up to 15m LOA or capable of speeds not in excess of 20km/h the requirement is as the French *Certificate C: Coches de Plaisance* – what the French call houseboats. The UK equivalent is the *Helmsman's Certificate of Competence (HOCC)* or the *International Certificate of Competence (ICC)*. For skippers of boats exceeding 15m LOA or capable of speeds in excess of 20km/h the requirement is as the French *Certificate PP: Péniches de Plaisance*, in other words barges converted into houseboats. There is no exact UK equivalent, but in practice the *Helmsman's Certificate of Competence* and the *International Certificate of Competence* are accepted. (It is also recommended to carry on board the CEVNI Rules: the *European Code for Inland Waterways*.)

Other general documentation is basic, sensible, desirable and predictable: everyone on board must have a valid passport and the ship's papers must be carried. Now, 'Ship's Papers' covers a multitude of possibilities: in general, you are not likely to be approached frequently, and when you are it will be to ask you for no more than the ship's Certificate of British Registry, be it from the standard Register of British Ships or from the Small Ships Register version.

In general, the permitted legal maximum dimensions for French inland waterways are as follows:

Length	38·5m	126' 3"	(converted down)
Beam	5·0m	16' 4"	
Draught	1·8m	5' 10"	
Air draught	3·5m	11' 5"	

This is not quite as straightforward as it might be, since the figures are all 'at best'. They take no account of the curves of bridges or the silted sides of canals; nor, of course, can they take into consideration the full width of the wheelhouse at its maximum air draught, the type of hull or the position of the propeller(s).

Two factors require serious thought before embarking on an expedition into the French canals: first the position and protection of props, and second the problems associated with deep-keel and bilge-keel craft. One central prop is in no danger, but is not of much help when manoeuvring in the tight circumstances that frequently prevail in the locks – and sometimes in the canals themselves. Twin props overcome the manoeuvring problems, but at the cost of vulnerability. Unfortunately, exposed props are a liability, and bilge keels a really doubtful proposition.

Their first encounter with the French canals can come to many UK boaters as something of a shock. The chances are that the cause of the shock lies not in the Frenchness of the canals, but in the very essence of canals as such; that it is, in fact, their first encounter with a canal of any kind. There can be little doubt that most skippers, crews and boats would benefit from a short encounter with British inland waterways before 'going foreign'. However, I have found it intriguing that many UK skippers who adamantly refuse even to consider cruising English canals seem to lose their critical faculties when afloat on the French waterways. It would seem that ceremony,

SIGNS ON FRENCH WATERWAYS

LOCK SIGNALS

No entry

Opening soon

Enter now

Lock not in operation

SOUNDS

— —	Attention
•	I am turning to starboard
••	I am turning to port
•••	I am going astern
••••	I am incapable of manoeuvring
•••••	Danger of collision
— — — —	(repeated) Distress signal
— •	I am turning round to starboard
— ••	I am turning round to port

WARNING SIGNS (RED)

or red lights
No entry

No overtaking

No passing

No long-term mooring

No anchoring

No mooring

No turning

Making waves forbidden

Pleasure craft forbidden

Rowing boats forbidden

Mandatory direction sign

Stop

Speed limit (km/h)

Sound horn

Danger

Major waterway ahead

Height (m)

Depth (m)

Width (m)

Keep away from bank (m)

VHF 11
Must contact waterways staff by radio

Channel is 40m from the right bank

Cross to left-hand side

Cross to right-hand side

Keep on right-hand side

Keep on left-hand side

Head for left-hand side

Head for right-hand side

 or
Do not cause wash

Motor boats forbidden

Keep out of port and tributary

Keep within limits (red)

OTHER SIGNS (BLUE)

or green lights
Entry allowed (green)

Electricity cable

Weir

Ferry

Side turning

Turning place

Anchoring place

Mooring place (long term)

Advisory direction sign

End of prohibited area

Junctions or crossings of secondary waterways

Priority waterway ahead (junction or crossing)

Keep within limits (green)

custom, culture and climate are all against such prior experimentation. Most of the disaster tales concern inexperienced skippers and crews – often those who have hired a boat for a fortnight, never having been on the water before.

THE KEY TO LOCKS

On the Seine, the Oise and the Paris canals (with the exception of three radar-observed semi-automatic locks on the St-Denis canal) keepers operate the locks, and are very prepared to tell you what to do. Sometimes they will help, and they will always come to your rescue if necessary. In the larger Seine locks (that is, up to Montereau) there are pegs and hooks and all kinds of devices to hang your rope on, but generally these are too far apart to be of use to small boats. When locking up, keep the lines taut at all times, as there is often quite a bit of turbulence when the sluices start. When locking down, slacken off as you descend with the water level. Watch out for nicks and niches in walls, stone walls, or steel-buffer-lined walls in locks; they can trap ropes disastrously, like a vice. Have a knife and an axe at the ready. If the rope jams, cast off or chop off immediately or you will 'hang' for a few minutes before tearing the fittings out.

RULES OF THE ROAD

Navigation lights and signals are in accordance with standard international regulations; 'right bank' and 'left bank' always refer to going downstream, towards the sea.

Commercial traffic always has priority over pleasure boats. This means avoiding all working vessels and giving way at difficult reaches or bridges, and certainly at lock entrances. Boats going downstream always have right of way over those going up. The rule of the road is keep right, and pass to port, but some *péniches* keep to the inside of the channel to avoid the stream. Craft doing this should show a blue flag on the right of the wheelhouse, or a flashing white light at night. Traffic proceeds at about 15m from the bank, at a maximum speed of 10km/h relative to the bank (8km/h for boats over 2,000 tons). Mooring along the banks is forbidden, except in case of emergency or fog.

BETWEEN ROUEN AND THE SEA

Now, many readers will have craft that are able to cross the Channel at a speedier rate of knots than the six or seven usually achieved by *Valcon*, but once on the Seine, no matter what their size or speed, all vessels are governed by the traffic movement regulations. 30 to 40 knots is of no avail once you are steaming up the river. Speed through the water is one thing, but speed over the ground can be, of course, something entirely different. Cruising up the Seine, progress is affected by the use the skipper makes (or fails to make) of the tide. In summer, you can always steam direct to Rouen on one tide in 20km/h (11 knots) craft, especially with a favourable current, which can achieve a very powerful 5 knots. Nevertheless, a study of sunrise and tide times enables you to choose the best combination of tides and daylight hours to suit your convenience. Please see the accompanying tables for details.

Leisure craft should keep outside the northern limit of the marked channel while downstream of the Tancarville bridge. Even at the lowest tides there is always 2m water within 50m of the buoys, and generally as far out as 200m. Going upstream to Rouen from the Tancarville bridge, craft keep to starboard, tending to the bank, and stay within 20m of the buoys marking the channel. Speed limits are as follows: from the estuary to Bouille (PK 260) 28km/h; from Bouille (PK 260) to Jeanne d'Arc bridge (Rouen) 14km/h.

TIME AND TIDE

The river is tidal for the 160km to the first lock at Poses-Amfreville. The water is salt up to the neighbourhood of the village of Aizier (PK 323). This influences fishing and the draught of boats, which ride from 2% to 3% deeper in fresh water. In the Baie de Seine the tide rises for about 5 hours from LW to HW, stands for 2–3 hours after HW, then falls for 5 hours. This vertical oscillation of the sea sends twice-daily 'waves' of HW up the river, so that the times of HW and LW travel upstream at about 14 knots. The wave as it travels becomes distorted, so that at any given point in the river the level rises for 1½–4½ hours, stands for 2½ hours, then falls for 5½–8½ hours.

Similarly, the time at which the stream turns becomes later as you pass upriver. At any given point below Rouen the tide floods for 3½–4½ hours and ebbs for 8–9 hours, but a boat can follow the flood upriver. All times are subject to modification by meteorological conditions and the amount of land water in the river. Spring rates are 6 knots on the flood and 4 knots on the ebb between Tancarville and Caudebec and about 3 knots above. Neap rates are two thirds.

Rouen, although only 53 miles (85km) in a straight line from the sea, is 78 miles (123km) by the meandering river. By timing its departure from the river mouth, however, even a 4-knot boat can complete the trip in 10 to 11 hours, carrying a flood tide all the way.

If you start from the river mouth at or shortly after the start of the flood, you can carry a fair tide all the way to Rouen. If you start too late or your boat is too slow or you idle on the way, you will be overtaken by the ebb tide and will have to anchor in the river. Coming downstream a period of flood tide must be encountered, and ebb cannot be carried all the way. While it is true that the ebb runs for all of 8–9 hours at any given point, as you descend on the ebb the forward wave of the approaching flood tide is coming upstream to meet you. If your boat is slow you may as well anchor to save fuel, as the tide will begin to ebb in 3½–4½ hours. In a fast boat it is worth battling on against the flood, as the further downriver you go the sooner the ebb starts.

Night travel by pleasure boats is prohibited, between 30 minutes after sunset and 30 minutes before sunrise, between Rouen and the sea. On some stretches of the French waterways leisure craft are permitted to navigate at night, but this is impossible if you have to pass through locks that are closed. My experience is that it is best for leisure craft not to navigate either at night or in fog or other serious weather conditions. In times of flood the authorities can close down the navigation, and that settles any personal decision-making. But in times of high winds, for example, protected stretches can be quiet and tempting, after which you need only to negotiate a ninety-degree bend to find you are in short sharp shockers that test your stowage and skills more than somewhat – especially where there is little room to move out of a narrow channel.

Craft are technically permitted to navigate in both fog and floods, but it must be deemed unwise. There is always some risk of collision, and during floods many dangerous encumbrances may be submerged. Often it will be impossible to distinguish the channel, and consequently you will risk running aground.

Fog is a frequent hazard in the mornings even in summer, occurring on about 10% of days between March and September, but in general floods are likely only between November and March. In very cold winters some canals freeze over, especially in the north, but generally only between December and February. Except when the river is flooded, normal levels (*RN, Retenue Normale*) are maintained by the navigation authorities. Often these are bettered by some centimetres to ensure that grounding does not occur in those stretches where silt is able to build up because of insufficient dredging, and air draught is consequently reduced by that amount. When the river is in flood, levels may reach their highest (*PHEN, Plus Hautes Eaux Navigables*), and at such times air draught is even less. Notices are posted at locks and navigation offices when *PHEN* has been reached. During periods of drought the depths of some canals can be reduced, often to the point of making navigation impossible in cases of extremely dry weather.

Water sports are prohibited between the sea and Rouen. In most other places they are allowed out of the channel, and there are special areas actually set aside for these activities. Sailing is allowed between the sea and Rouen provided that it does not impede commercial traffic, which has absolute right of way (note that 'impeding' a cargo ship also means making it slow down or even hesitate). Travelling between Rouen and the sea under sail is not to be recommended – you are bound to get in the way of merchant ships, and it is a long, tiring journey involving several overnight stops in the Seine. Moreover, the adverse currents can reach 6 knots.

VHF

Craft over 20m LOA must have VHF Ch 6, 13, 16 and 73.
Le Havre Port, Rouen Port, and Honfleur Radar listen on Ch 16.
Between Rouen and the sea, leisure craft listen on Ch 73.

Radio links with port and navigation services

Call sign	Call Ch	Work Ch
Le Havre Radar	16	12 or 20
Le Havre Port	16	12 or 20
Pilote Le Havre	12	12
Radar Honfleur	16 or 73	73, 13, 74, or 10
Rouen Port	73 or 11	73 or 11
Pilote Rouen	16 or 73	73 or 11

River traffic uses mainly Ch 10, but also 6, 8, 72 and 77

VHF LINKS WITH FRANCE TELECOM

Location	Direct dialling	Manual connection
Le Havre – The Seine estuary downstream from Quillebeuf (PK 330)	62, 84	23, 26, 28
Rouen Aval – (downstream Rouen) from Tancarville to Rouen (PK 340 to PK 240)	1, 86	25, 27, 64
Rouen Amont – Rouen to Bonnières (PK 250 to PK 140)	85, 87	24
Substations of the Paris public radiotelephone service (☎ 04 42 46 72 22)		
Paris Aval – Vernon to Paris (PK 150 to PK 0)	28, 84	23, 26
Paris – Paris and suburbs, Mont Valérien	82	25, 27
Villejuif	83	25, 27

RADIOTELEPHONES

It is possible to have on board your boat a radiotelephone system that, thanks to a special service, allows you to connect with the national and international phone network either manually or automatically, according to the type of system you opt for.

To install a radiotelephone on board your boat, you must contact an authorised installer (a list of whom is available from France Telecom in Saint Lys; ☎ 05 61 19 36 36. Operating licences and all official certificates necessary for carrying an on-board radiotelephone can be obtained from France Telecom inspectors, marine radio sector.

To call a boat with a phone aboard, dial 06 It is possible that you will have problems getting through to your party (if he is not within range of a relay station, or if his boat phone is not on standby).

It is possible to call a boat (assuming the phone is on standby) through the interme-
diary of several public relay services:
Boulogne Radio ☎ 03 21 33 25 26 (Nord, Ile de France, Normandie, Est, Alsace)
Marseille Radio ☎ 04 91 73 11 14 (Rhône Valley, Midi)
Arcachon Radio ☎ 05 56 83 40 50 (Gironde)
Saint-Nazaire ☎ 02 40 91 04 00 (Ouest)
Boats equipped with radiotelephones are listed in the *Official Directory of Boats Par-
taking of Waterways Services,* which is available at the Centre de Repartition et de
Vente des Annuaires, 5, rue Emile Baudot, 91308 Massy ☎ 03 60 11 52 00.
In the event of technical problems, contact the Renseignements Radiomaritimes at
31470 Saint Lys ☎ 05 61 19 36 00, or dial toll free ☎ 0800 19 20 21.

ADMINISTRATION

After much changing of minds and attitudes, VNF (Voies Navigables de France)
seem to have reached something of a compromise with the representatives of French
leisure-craft owners. Presently, the situation is as follows:

Voies Navigables de France, VNF, is the public body which takes responsibility for
maintaining, running and developing most of the 8,500km of canals and canalised
rivers which flow through France. Over and above the main axes of waterborne trans-
port, many different routes are now kept busy thanks to leisure users.

So as to promote this activity, VNF has set itself the priority of improving the service throughout the network which it looks after. The development of river-going
tourism will require changes in the existing equipment to suit leisure-boat travel. This
is why VNF has decided to concentrate its efforts this year on installing equipment to
make travel more comfortable. Water supply points and household waste containers
will be provided. At the same time the leisure-boat travellers will be consulted, making it possible to draw up a programme for equipping the river network with more
elaborate services (toilets, washing and shower facilities, telephones etc.), to which
users would have access.

The network needs to be well maintained and well run to achieve an overall improvement in services. This is financed by contributions from all the users. For leisure-boat users, this contribution will take the form of a statutory payment or toll.

The toll must be paid by all leisure-boat owners. Light craft of 5 metres length and
under, with a motor of less than 9·9CV in real terms (that is, 7·29kw), as well as all
manually propelled boats, are exempt from payment.

The toll is due each time the boat travels on waterways entrusted to VNF; it gives
the right to normal use of waterways in the public domain. By boat travel we understand boat movements, whether or not the boat passes through a lock.

The toll is not refundable and does not exempt the user from:
• payment for certain extra services such as going through underground passages in
  a tug convoy, use of lifts, sloping water sections ... or going through locks outside
  normal boating hours;
• mooring fees, especially in ports, or for certain docking facilities which offer leisure
  users specialised services.

When you pay the toll, you will receive a certificate of payment and a sticker which
must be shown when required. The toll sticker must be placed at the front of the boat,
on the starboard side so that it can be seen from outside, under all circumstances.

Checking-up operations may be carried out at any point in the network by official
representatives of the VNF, the navigation services and the police.

In the event of infringement, a police report will be drawn up. Those who contra-
vene the regulations will be liable to pay a fine as laid down in the legislation, or could
in certain cases and after the agreement of the chief prosecutor of the French Republic

pay a negotiated fine.

The toll sticker is available directly at one of the VNF centres, payable by cheque made out to Voies Navigables de France, in cash, or by bank transfer (VNF Béthune Siège, bank code 10071. Code of cashier's desk: 62100 Bank, account number 10003010 584 key 14.)

The simplest way is to pay the toll by post, sending it to the VNF centre of your choice. You must enclose the following with your payment:

- the owner's name and address
- the name of the boat
- the outside to outside length and width of the hull
- the registration number, the enrolment number or at least the series number
- the type of toll desired – and the dates for the 'holiday' rate
- a stamped envelope with your address

If possible, produce or enclose a photocopy of the navigation permit, a sea card or a corresponding registration document, as well as proof of the motor's power. A receipt will be given on request.

In the case of the 'leisure' rate, the user must date and sign one of the 30 spaces on the back of the toll card for each day of river travel. The back of the toll card must always be visible from the outside. The current rates are as follows. The prices are in French Francs:

	I	II	III	IV	V
	12m	12–25m	25–40m	40–60m	60+m
Yearly	450	650	1,300	2,100	2,600
Leisure 30 days	250	450	800	1,250	1,550
Holiday 15 days	100	200	300	400	500

VNF CENTRES

The relevant addresses and telephone numbers of the VNF centres are given below. They can also provide a list of lock closures (chômages).

Head Office (payment by post)
Béthune 175 rue Ludovic Boutleux, 62408 Béthune Cedex
☎ 03 21 63 24 24 *Fax* 03 21 63 24 42
Agde
Service de la Navigation de Toulouse
☎ 04 67 94 10 99
Ecluse ronde d'Agde, 34304 Agde
☎ 04 67 94 23 09
Arles
1 quai Gare Maritime, 13637 Arles
☎ 04 90 96 00 85
Béthune
Chemin du Halage, 62400 Béthune
☎ 03 21 57 63 37

Calais
45 quai de la Meuse, 62100 Calais
☎ 03 21 34 25 58
Chalon/Saône
Port fluvial, 71100 Chalon
☎ 03 85 43 20 10

Conflans
Cours de Chimay, 76700 Conflans
☎ 01 39 72 73 09
Douai
319 bd Paul Hayez
☎ 03 27 87 21 67
Dunkerque
Terre-plein du Jeu de Mail, 59140 Dunkerque
☎ 03 28 25 30 78
Le Havre
La Citadelle av. Lucien Corbeaux, 76600 Le Havre
☎ 02 35 22 99 34
Lyon
Quai Marechal Joffre, 69002 Lyon
☎ 04 78 42 74 99
Marseille/Aubigny
Ecluse d'Aubigny, BP2, 18320 Marseille
☎ 02 48 76 41 95

Port St-Louis
Ecluse Maritime, 13230 Port St-Louis
☎ 04 42 48 41 94
Reims
11 bd Paul Doumer, 51084 Reims
☎ 03 26 85 75 95
St-Jean-de-Losne
17 quai National, BP 16, 21170 St-Jean-de
Losne
☎ 03 80 29 01 37
Saint-Mammès
11 Quai du Loing, 77670 Saint-Mammès
☎ 64 70 57 70
Saint-Quentin
2 av. Leo Lagrange, 02100 Saint-Quentin
☎ 03 23 62 60 21
Sète
1 Quai Philippe Regy, 34200 Sète
☎ 04 67 46 35 70
Valenciennes
24 chemin du Halage, 59300 Valenciennes
☎ 03 27 46 44 60
Vitry-le-François
La Citadelle, BP 403 – 51308 Vitry
☎ 03 26 74 60 94

INFORMATION AND GUIDES

You will find a wide selection of maps, books and guides on French waterways to help you organise your stay and discover historical monuments, local cuisine, and special products. If you wish to prolong your holiday dream on water, art books, novels, travel books, posters and postcards are also available. To spread information about all the possibilities offered by waterways, VNF co-edits with Editions Danae the *Fluvial Tourism Directory-Handbook*. Where to rent a houseboat, which the most remarkable sites on the Canal de Bourgogne are, which lakes can be used for windsurfing, or where one can stop and fill up with fresh water or petrol: you will find the answers to all your questions, as well as practical information and techniques, and, above all, ideas for tourist itineraries, both picturesque and often little known.

Orders and enquiries to Librairie Maritime et d'Outremer, 17 Rue Jacob, 75006 Paris. ☎ 01 46 33 47 48 *Fax* 01 43 29 96 77.

Generally helpful guides

Le Tourisme Fluviale en France foc
Mieux vivre le Tourisme Fluvial en France foc
Both available from VNF (Voies Navigables de France)
Another generally useful publication with up-to-date information is *Fluvial*, a bimonthly magazine published at 64 rue Jean-Jacques Rousseau, 21000 Dijon. ☎ 03 80 73 39 39.

The Mairie de Paris publishes an excellent pilot guide, and a first-rate folding map covering the three Paris waterway systems. The first is *Le réseau fluvial de la Ville de Paris: guide du plaisancier* and the second is the *Carte*. Copies of both can be obtained free of charge from:
Bureaux de la 1ère Circonscription
5 quai de la Loire, 75019 Paris
☎ 01 42 08 30 91/01 44 89 15 15 *Fax* 01 44 89 15 16.
Bureaux de la 2ème Circonscription
6 av. Gallieni, 77100 Meaux
☎ 01 60 09 53 90 *Fax* 01 60 09 57 80
Port de Plaisance de Paris-Arsenal
11 bd de la Bastille, 75012 Paris
☎ 01 43 41 39 32 *Fax* 01 44 74 02 66

Useful addresses, contacts and information

Comité Regional de Tourisme d'Ile de France, 73–75 rue Cambronne, 75015 Paris, ☎ 01 45 67 89 41
Comité Départemental de Tourisme de Seine-Maritime, 2 bis rue Petit Salut, BP 680, 76000 Rouen Cèdex, ☎ 02 35 88 61 32
Comité Départemental du Tourisme et des Loisirs, Hôtel du Département, 2 Le Campus, 95032 Cergy-Pontoise Cédex, ☎ 05 05 34 25 32 53
Office de Tourisme de Paris, 127 av. des Champs Elysées 75008 Paris, ☎ 01 49 52 53 54
Comité Départemental de Tourisme de Seine Saint Denis, 2 rue de la Légion d'Honneur, 93200 Saint Denis, ☎ 01 42 43 33 55

GEAR

'Fenders must float. Tyres are only allowed if they have an inner tube, inflated so that they will float. Fix them in place with two crossed ropes tied to two different points on the boat.' That is the legal position, but the general working attitude is not so strict. A plank/ladder is a boon in the upper reaches of the Seine, permitting access to the bank when you cannot moor up close enough. Other mooring necessities are: four 20m lengths of good rope and many shorter ones, two strong sound boathooks, two land anchors, a big sharp axe and a heavy hammer, and two strong sharp knives. Water intake filters need to be really efficient and easy to get at. Sea toilets are technically illegal in France, and chemical ones are a requirement.

A reasonably powerful engine is essential. Petrol (*essence*) is no problem: you pay the going rate wherever you happen to be, and there are always plenty of accessible points. But diesel (*gasoil*) is another matter. The upper Seine is short of diesel fuel points, so it is always a good idea to fill up whenever you have the chance. Then there is the question of the legality of Red or White. This is the official position as outlined by VNF: 'Fuel: A 1976 law forbids the use of certain types of fuel, considered harmful to the environment, in the motors of pleasure craft. Fuel in the internal fuel tanks of boats entering France from another country is not subject to customs duty.'

At most marinas and *haltes* there is mains water and power: the standard French two-pin points. A bicycle is an excellent idea if you have the space – but most of the time on the Seine you will be within walking distance of all you need, and a cluttered boat is a pain. Binoculars are needed for conning locks, bridges, bread shops and wine cellars.

FISHING IN FRESH WATER

Before trying to hook any fish, sportsmen must mandatorily:

- become members of an AAPP – Association Agréé de Pêche et de Pisciculture (official anglers' club) and have the required membership card, which is personal and annual;
- pay one of the above for a licence corresponding to the type of fishing they intend to do.

Certain local fishing associations have made with neighbouring AAPPs reciprocal agreements whereby fishing possibilities are increased (inquire locally). When a fisherman belongs to many associations, the fishing fee is due only once. Until 16 years of age, minors are not obliged to pay the fishing tax, as long as they use only one line with a maximum of two hooks (casting excluded).

What you have to know:

- in order to ensure healthful reproduction of the fish population, fishing is forbidden during certain periods of the year;
- specific laws make it forbidden to fish for some types of fish, in order to protect certain species;
- rules for catch, minimum lengths for certain species and forbidden types of fishing are established by and published in an official decree;
- during fishing season, fishing is permitted from 30 minutes before sunrise until 30 after sunset.

The tourist fisherman is advised to find out beforehand the specifics of fishing regulations in the waters he intends to fish by calling on:

- local police authorities;
- agriculture and forest authorities (Directions Départementales de l'Agriculture et de la Forêt);
- waterways authorities (Directions Départementales de l'Equipment et aux Services de Navigation);

- local town halls (official decrees are posted there);
- local branches of the AAPP;
- official fishing organisations and bait and tackle shop owners.

LOCKS EQUIPPED WITH VHF

Ablon Ch 22
Amfreville Ch 18
Andresy Ch 22
Boran sur Oise Ch 18
Bougival Ch 22
Champagne Ch 18
Chatou Ch 18
Coudray Ch 22
Evry Ch 18
Grande-Bosse Ch 22
Janville Ch 22
La Cave Ch 22
L'Isle Adam Ch 22

Marolles Ch 18
Méricourt Ch 18
Notre Dame de la Garenne Ch 22
Pontoise Ch 18
Port à l'Anglais Ch 18
Suresnes Ch 22
Tancarville Ch 18
Varenne Ch 22
Venette Ch 18
Vives Eaux Ch 18

River traffic uses mainly Ch 10, but also 6, 8, 72 and 77

PARIS VHF RADIO

	VHF Ch
Port de Plaisance de Paris-Arsenal	09
Canal St-Martin	
la Villette (1/2) Temple (7/8)	20
Canal St-Denis	
la Briche (7) Flandre (1)	20
Seine Security	12

LIMITING DIMENSIONS

THE RIVERS SEINE AND OISE	Distance	Locks	Depth	Height	Length	Width
The Seine	km	m	m	m	m	m
Le Havre to Rouen: tidal seaway						
navigation	105	0				
Rouen to Paris	233	6	3·50	6·90	180·00	11·40
Paris to Marcilly	174	19				
Paris to Montereau			2·80	5·50	180·00	11·40
Montereau to La Grande Bosse			2·80	5·50	180·00	11·40
La Grande Bosse to Bray			2·20	5·50	90·00	11·40
Bray to Nogent			1·80	4·35	45·00	7·50
Nogent to Marcilly			1·40	3·75	38·50	7·50
Canal de Tancarville	25	1	3·50	7·00	185·00	23·00
Canal St-Denis	7	7	4·60	2·60	61·50	8·00
Canal St-Martin	5	9	4·37	1·90	40·70	7·70
Canal and river l'Ourcq	108	10				
Paris to Pavillons-sous-Bois			4·07	2·60		
Pavillons-sous-Bois to Port aux Pêches			2·40	0·80		

PARIS

	St-Martin	St-Denis	Major Ourcq	Minor Ourcq
Length (km)	4·5	6·6	11·1	97
Width (m)	27	30	18–24	10–11
LOA (m)	25·28	28·45		15·5
Air draught (m)	4·27	4·44	4·04	2·4
Draught (m)	1·9	2·6–31	2·6	0·82

1. Moving slowly and strictly adhering to the main channel.
2. Possible 1·1m – but only at users' risk.

OURCQ – GRANDE SECTION

PK	Place
0	Bassin de la Villette
3	Pantin
5	Bobigny
8	Bondy
10	Pavillons-sous-Bois

OURCQ – PETITE SECTION

13·5	Ecluse de Sevran
31·9	Ecluse de Fresnes-sur-Marne
40·3	Ecluse de Vignely
47	Ecluse de Villenoy
54·9	Ecluse de Meaux-St-Lazare
64·7	Ecluse de Varreddes
97	Ecluse de Mareuil-sur-Ourcq
99·7	Ecluse de Queue-d'Ham
103	Ecluse de Marolles
104·1	Ecluse de La Ferté-Millon

USEFUL ADDRESSES – AUTHORITIES, BOATING AND TOURISM

SEINE

Navigation sub-divisions

Nogent-Sur-Seine, Ècluse de Nogent, 10400 ☎ 03 25 39 86 48

Melun, 26 quai H. Rossignol, 77500 ☎ 01 64 30 54 22

Joinville ☎ 01 43 75 66 53

Paris, 2 quai de la Tournelle, 75005 ☎ 01 44 41 16 80

Suresnes, 27 quai Gallieni, 92150 ☎ 01 45 06 21 58

Bougival, Ecluse, 78380 ☎ 01 39 69 82 33

Andresy ☎ 01 34 64 02 26

Limay, 62 route du Hazay, 78250 ☎ 01 30 92 56 00

Poses-Amfreville, Ecluse de Poses, BP 3, 27590 Pitres ☎ 02 32 49 80 19

Rouen, 71 av. J. Chastellain, 76000 ☎ 02 35 89 44 72

Port Autonome de Rouen, 34 bd de Boisquilbert, BP 4075, 76022 Rouen Cédex ☎ 02 35 52 54 00

Port Autonome du Havre, Terre plein de la Barre, BP 1413, 76067 Le Havre Cédex ☎ 02 35 21 74 00

Nogent-sur-Seine 10400
Boating
Beck-Barbuise Courtovent, ☎ 03 25 21 40 57
Tourist
Comité du Tourisme Nogentais, ☎ 01 60 67 23 52

Bray-sur-Seine
Boating
Garage du Quai, 9 quai de l'Ile, ☎ 01 60 67 10 56

Montereau-Faut-Yonne 77130
Boating
Ets Andre Martin, 14 rue Gue-Pucelle, ☎ 01 64 32 14 28
Ets J. B. Chapus, 19 rue de la Pepinière Royale, ☎ 01 64 32 02 43

St-Mammès 77670
Boating
Vedettes du Val de Seine, 5 quai du Loing, ☎ 01 60 70 18 18
J. Jolivet, 31 rue des Sablonnieres, ☎ 01 64 23 19 07
Tourist
Place Samois, BP15, 77250 Moret sur Loing, ☎ 01 60 70 41 66

Veneux-les-Sablons 77250 Moret sur Loing
Boating
Rousseau, Quai du Loing, ☎ 60 70 52 87

Thomery
Boating
Chantier Barat, 35 rue Royale Samoreau

Tourist
35 rue Royale, 77210 Avon, ☎ 01 43 46 55 53

Fontainebleau-Avon 77300
Boating
Roques et Lecoeur, 246 rue Grande, ☎ 01 64 22 12 35
Tourist
31 place Napoleon Bonaparte, ☎ 01 64 22 25 68

Valvins 77210 Avon
Boating
Ets Golletto Volvins, ☎ 01 60 72 14 60

Vaux-le-Penil 77000 Melun
Boating
Same 1240, av. Saint-Just Z. I de Melun

Melun 77000
Boating
Port de Plaisance Stephane Mallarme CCI Melun, rue Bancel, ☎ 01 64 52 45 01
Seine Loing Rivières, 42 rue Bancel, ☎ 01 64 52 45 01
Tourist
av. Gallieni, ☎ 01 64 37 11 31

Dammarie-les-Lys 77190
Boating
Ste Jouan, 494 av. Anatole France

Boissise-le-Roi
Boating
Port de Plaisance du Roi, rue Olivieri, ☎ 01 64 09 84 95

Morsang sur Seine 91250
Boating
Chantier Naval Klein, 13 chemin des Iles, ☎ 01 60 75 01 09

Saintry sur Seine 91100 Corbeil Essonnes
Boating
Port Saintry, 138 route de Morsang, ☎ 01 60 75 49 34

Corbeil Essonnes 91100
Boating
Genevois, 1108 quai Bourgoin, ☎ 01 64 96 02 70
Ets Cordon, 49 bd Kennedy, ☎ 01 64 96 06 83
Marceau, 102 rue du Bas Coudray, ☎ 01 60 88 08 38
Tourist
4 place Vaillant Couturier, ☎ 01 64 96 23 97

Evry 91000
Boating
Bougie Champion, 20 allée du Vivarais, ☎ 01 60 77 75 25
Produits Durieu S.A., Z.A.I. La Marinière Bondoufle, ☎ 01 60 77 28 70
Tourist
Hall Information Agora, Cours Monseigneur Romero, ☎ 01 64 97 23 82

Soisy sur Seine 91450
Boating
Quick Nautic, 15 rue Paul Franchi
M. Boudry, ☎ 01 60 75 64 80

Ris-Orangis 91130
Boating
Jomo Sports, Centre Commercial de l'Aunette, rue Provence R.N. 7, ☎ 01 69 43 01 90

Grigny 91350
Boating
Sports Nautiques, 25 R.N. 7, ☎ 01 69 06 99 09

Draveil 191210
Boating
Port aux Cerises, ☎ 01 69 42 46 76/69 40 33 10
Tourist
97 bd Henri Barbusse, ☎ 01 69 03 09 39

Viry-Chatillon 91170
Boating
Sietam Roulev, 42–48 av. Pdt Kennedy, ☎ 01 69 84 24 00

Savigny sur Orge 91600
Tourist
17 rue Jacques Coeur, ☎ 01 69 05 34 20

Longjumeau 91160
Tourist
6 bis rue Leontine Sohier, ☎ 01 64 54 19 67

Juvisy sur Orge 91260
Boating
Base de loisirs – Centre nautique, Grand Garage de l'Essonne, 137 av. du General de Gaulle, R.N. 7 Viry-Chatillon, ☎ 01 69 21 35 90
Tourist
Place du General Leclerc, ☎ 01 69 45 76 09

Villeneuve-St-Georges 94190
Boating
Base Nautique de Villeneuve triage 19 av. de Choisy, ☎ 01 43 89 04 64

Choisy-le-Roi 94600
Boating
Chantiers Navals de la Seine, Ets Marguerrie, 51 quai Pompadour, ☎ 01 48 90 90 11
Tourist
8 place de l'Eglise, ☎ 01 48 84 01 91

Alfortville 94140
Boating
Scabott, BP 132, ☎ 01 43 78 28 28

CANAL SAINT MARTIN/CANAL ST DENIS
Navigation sub-divisions
Canal Saint Martin 1ère Circonscription: 5 quai de la Loire, 75019 Paris ☎ 01 42 08 30 91
Canal Saint Denis 1ère Circonscription: 5 quai de la Loire, 75019 Paris ☎ 01 42 08 30 91

CANAL DE L'OURCQ
Navigation sub-divisions
From PK 0 to PK 11 Canal de l'Ourcq to Grand Gabarit
1ère Circonscription: 5 quai de la Loire, 75019 Paris ☎ 01 42 08 30 91

From PK 11 to Petit Gabarit and river l'Ourcq
2ème Circonscription: 6 av. Gallieni, 77100 Meaux ☎ 01 60 09 53 90

Bassin de la Villette
Boating
Section des Canaux, 6 quai de la Seine, 75019 Paris, ☎ 01 44 89 14 14
Canauxrama, 13 quai de la Loire, 75019 Paris, ☎ 01 42 39 15 00
Paris Canal, 11 quai de la Loire, 75019 Paris, ☎ 42 40 96 97
HBI Ourcq Loisirs, Pantin 93500, ☎ 01 40 38 95 35
Tourist
25 ter rue du Pre St-Gervais, ☎ 01 48 44 93 72

Bobigny 93000
Tourist
125 bis rue Jean Jaurès, ☎ 01 48 30 63 02

Livry-Gargan 93190
Tourist
5 place de l'Hôtel de Ville, ☎ 02 43 30 61 60

Claye-Souilly 77410
Boating
Sinope Evasion, ☎ 01 60 27 05 51/01 46 82 15 29
SM Marine, ☎ 01 64 34 63 17

Meaux 77100
Boating
Section des Canaux, 6 av. Gallieni, ☎ 01 60 09 53 90

CROSSING PARIS
Boating
Port de l'Arsenal, 11 bd de la Bastille, 75012 Paris, ☎ 01 43 41 39 32
Port des Champs-Elysées, Quai de la Concorde, 75008 Paris, ☎ 01 42 65 90 70
M. Colin Intens, Port de Javel Haut, 75015 Paris, ☎ 01 40 59 86 89
Bateaux Mouche, Pont de l'Alma Port de la Conference, 75008 Paris, ☎ 01 42 25 96 10
Vedettes Paris Ile-de-France, Port de Suffren 75007 Paris, ☎ 01 47 05 71 29/01 44 18 08 03
Ste Vedettes du Pont Neuf, Square du Vert Galant 75001 Paris, ☎ 01 46 33 98 38
Quiztour, 19 rue d'Athène 75009 Paris, ☎ 01 45 26 05 03
Les Bateaux Parisiens, Port de la Bourdonnais, 75007 Paris, ☎ 01 44 11 33 44
Boating diesel Bateau Cher M. Losalle, Quai d'Austerlitz 75013 Paris, ☎ 01 45 85 28 92
Boating engineer Flotte Française, 21 rue des Filles du Calvaire, 75003 Paris, ☎ 01 42 72 95 00
Tourist
127 av. des Champs-Elysées, 75008 Paris, ☎ 01 01 49 52 53 54

NAVIGATION FROM PARIS TO THE SEA

Issy-les-Moulineaux 92130
Boating
Aerazur, 58 bd Gallieni, ☎ 01 41 23 24 25
Hurt France S.A.R.L., 37 rue C. Desmoulins, ☎ 01 45 57 12 61

Boulogne-Billancourt 92100
Boating
Chant au Vent, Evasion, Ste Nautic Croisiere, ☎ 01 46 21 48 15
Européenne de Navigation, Quai du Point du Jour, ☎ 01 41 10 86 90
Marine Service, Quai du 4 Septembre (face au 1)
Mazura Marine, Quai A. Le Gallo (face au 36), ☎ 01 46 05 04 04/0 146 05 69 98
Paris Yacht Chandler peniche PYC, Quai du 4 Septembre (face au 9), ☎ 01 48 25 15 06

Saint-Cloud 92210
Boating
Marina Passerelle de l'Avre, ☎ 01 46 02 87 52
Helice Club de France, (face au 60) quai Carnot, ☎ 01 46 02 00 90
Nauti Hall (Guyard), 1432–1455 quai Marcel Dassault, ☎ 01 46 02 00 21

Suresnes 92150
Boating
Aglo S.A., 40 rue Carnot, ☎ 01 45 06 19 44
Tourist
50 bd Henri Sellier, ☎ 01 45 06 70 14

Puteaux 92800
Boating
Soprolor, 41 rue du Commandant Roland, BP 179, 93350 Le Bourget, ☎ 01 48 36 69 69

Courbevoie 92400
Boating
Ste Canots Kayoks Lagon, 81 rue Danton, ☎ 01 43 33 08 59
La Prairie, 36 bd A. Briand, ☎ 01 43 33 45 16
Lefol et Cie, 43 rue Louis Blanc
Les Materiaux Nauveaux, 108 rue de Caen, Musée Roybet-Fould

Neuilly sur Seine 92200
Boating
Societe 3B, 25 bd Vital Bouhot, ☎ 01 46 24 65 10
Yachting, 20 bis av. du General de Gaulle
France Motors, 166 av. du General de Gaulle, ☎ 01 46 24 96 10
Techni-France, 6 rue Louis Philippe, ☎ 01 47 47 79 06
SACM Diesel, 40 rue du Moulin des Bruyeres, 92400 Courbevoie, ☎ 01 47 17 11 11
Tourist
22 rue d'Orléans, ☎ 01 47 22 21 24

Levallois-Perret 92300
Boating
SK Diffusion, 43 rue Voltaire
Soportex, 123 av. Louis Roche BP 47, 92230 Gennevilliers, ☎ 01 47 94 42 18
Tubouto, 6 rue Paul Vaillant Couturier, ☎ 01 47 57 31 21

Asnières 92600
Port Van Gogh:
Boating
Nautic Motors France, Quai Dervaux (face au 73), ☎ 01 47 93 08 02/47 93 01 14
CFEC/Batteries, 77 rue de la Bongarde, 92233 Gennevilliers Cedex, ☎ 01 47 93 98 50
Dary S.A. 51 rue Jean Jaures, 92270 Bois Colombes
Suroil S.A. ☎ 01 40 86 98 00, 4 av. Laurent Cely

Clichy 92110
Boating
Mecanauti, 14 rue Chance-Milly, ☎ 01 42 70 08 32
Voilerie Le Noan, 155 bd V. Hugo, ☎ 01 47 37 14 55

St-Ouen 93400
Pieces Loisirs Distribution, 51 bd Biron
Ouvrord Villard et Guilux, 65 rue du Dr Bauer, ☎ 01 40 11 41 79
Perkins (moteurs), 9 av. Michelet, ☎ 01 40 10 42 43
Valeo distribution, 21 rue Blanqui, ☎ 01 49 45 32 32
Tourist
Place de la Republique, ☎ 01 40 11 77 36

St-Denis 93200
Boating
Collin S.A., 20 bd Carnot, ☎ 01 48 22 33 77
Sikkens, 164 rue Ambroise Croizat, ☎ 01 48 20 61 64
Tourist
Place Victor Hugo, ☎ 01 42 43 33 55

Villeneuve-la-Garenne 92390
Boating
Port sur Sley, 42 quai Alfred sur Sley, ☎ 01 47 98 22 43
Marie Louise, Mairie ☎ 01 47 98 18 52
Ets Theumier, 55 quai Alfred sur Sley, ☎ 01 47 94 53 56
Deyel, 35 quai d'Asnières, ☎ 01 40 85 10 10
Quim Galite Diffusion, 01 47 94 51 93, 172 bd Gallieni

Epinay sur Seine 93800
Boating
Michel Marine, 20 rue du Port, ☎ 01 42 35 07 75

Gennevilliers 92230
Boating
ARMT, 5 rue Edmond Darbois, ☎ 01 47 93 65 95
General Motors France, 56 av. L. Roche, 95100 Argenteuil, ☎ 01 40 80 70 00
KHO Deutz MWM, 115 rue du Fosse Blanc, ☎ 01 46 13 87 85
Serofim Le Carbone Lorraine, 37 rue Jean Jaurès BP 31, ☎ 47 99 98 41
Cie Francaise d'Electrochimie, 77–97 rue de la Bongarde BP 68, ☎ 01 47 93 45 10
Tourist
117 av. Gabriel Péri, ☎ 01 47 99 33 92

Argenteuil 95100
Boating

Arcus Barge Sauvetage

Colombes 92700
Boating
Topoplastic, 240 rue G. Peri, ☎ 01 42 42 39 14

Bois-Colombes 92270
Boating
Clanche, 143 rue V. Hugo, ☎ 01 47 81 91 17

Nanterre 92000
Boating
Airex France, 10–12 rue des Trois-Fontanot, ☎ 01 47 73 71 55
Elite Marine, 23 rue du Port, ☎ 01 47 25 33 31
Lucas Service France, 26–32 rue Lavoisier, BP 210, ☎ 01 47 25 92 84
SIA Dumoutier, 68 rue Alfred Dequeant, ☎ 01 47 82 96 74
Stop Fire, 164 av. G. Clemenceau, ☎ 01 42 04 58 08

Carrières sur Seine 78420
Boating
ACN Nautic, 161 av. Maurice Berteaux Sartrouville, ☎ 01 39 14 89 60

Rueil-Malmaison 92500
Boating
Ford Moteurs Industriels, 344 av. Napoleon Bonaparte, ☎ 01 47 32 60 00
Ciba-Geigy (Div MPA), 2 rue Lionel Terray, ☎ 47 52 30 00
Tourist
Parc Central, 160 av. Paul Doumer, ☎ 01 47 32 35 75

Chatou 78400
Tourist
Place de la Gare, ☎ 01 30 71 30 89

Bougival 78380
Tourist
Hôtel de Ville rue Joffre, ☎ 01 39 69 01 15

Houilles 78800
Boating
Chantier Naval Bisbal, 55 bd H. Barbusse, ☎ 01 39 68 60 69

Sartrouville 78500
Boating
SDM Electronique, 17–25 rue Barian, ☎ 01 39 14 68 33
Nautirama, 211 av. Maurice Berteaux, ☎ 01 39 13 21 52

Maisons-Laffitte 78600
Boating
Detroit Marine, 21 rue de la Digue
Tourist
Hôtel de Ville, 44 rue Guynemer, ☎ 0139 62 63 64

La Frette sur Seine 95530
Boating
Chevalier, 121 quai de Seine, ☎ 01 39 97 42 71

Herblay 95220
Boating
Chantier naval d'Achīres, La Croix-d'Achères, 78260 Acheres, ☎ 01 39 11 02 27
Pognon, 87 quai Gaillon, ☎ 01 39 19 75 72

Conflans Ste Honorine 78700
Boating
Ambience Yachting, Ile du Devant Port de Plaisance, ☎ 01 39 72 64 12/63 65
Ste Disselect, 125 quai de l'Ile au Bac
FIAT CL Auto, 19 rue Pasteur, ☎ 01 39 19 61 61
Auto-Choland (Delhay), 24 quai Gaillon, ☎ 01 39 19 82 52
Diesel Marine, 7 quai des Martyrs de la Resistance, ☎ 01 39 72 68 83
Integral Process, 36 quai Eugene Lecorre, ☎ 01 39 72 62 27/86 78
Tourist
23 rue Maurice Berteaux, ☎ 01 34 90 99 09
Centre de Yachting, ☎ 01 39 72 63 03

Andresy 78570
Boating
Carre Chantier Naval, 27 Ile des Migneaux, 78300 Poissy, ☎ 01 39 65 02 37
Wattelez, 18 rue Gerard Bongard, 78300 Poissy, ☎ 30 74 02 07

Carrières-sous-Poissy 78300
Boating
Marina, av. Vanderbilt, ☎ 01 30 74 38 46
AGD Strago S.A.R.L., 451 chemins des Grandes Terres, ☎ 39 65 41 35
Chantier Nautique, Ile des Migneaux, ☎ 01 39 65 02 37

Poissy 78300
Boating
Chantier naval Île des Migneaux, 27 Ile des Migneaux, ☎ 01 39 65 02 37
Tourist
132 rue du General de Gaulle, ☎ 01 30 74 60 65

Villennes sur Seine 78670
Boating
Nautisplus, 350 chemin de Poissy, ☎ 01 39 75 84 90

Triel sur Seine 78510
Boating
Chantier Nautique Mallard, 5 quai A. Briand, ☎ 01 39 65 60 73
Tourist
157 bis rue P. Doumer, ☎ 01 39 75 05 38

Meulan 78250
Boating
Relais Nautique de Meulan, 8 rue Bignon, ☎ 01 34 74 02 51
Fluestour Yvelines, ☎ 01 34 75 11 36

Porcheville 78440 Gargenville
Boating
Chantiers du Vexin, 22 bd julien Bouriailliat

Limay 78520
Boating
Chantier Naval, 47 Quai aux Vins, ☎ 01 34 77 20 85
Galais, 15 route Nationale, ☎ 01 34 77 02 78
Marine Loisirs, 7 rue G. Clemenceau

Rosny sur Seine 78710
Boating
Steacma, Clos de Malassis, ☎ 01 30 42 89 00

General 73

Freneuse 78840
Boating
Hall Marine, 5 rue Nationale, ☎ 01 30 93 07 10
R.G.F., 5 R.N. 13 (Remorque), ☎ 30 97 18 87

Bonnières sur Seine 78270
Boating
Ponton Plaisance, Camp de loisirs, ☎ 01 30 93 31 93
Port St-Nicolas, ☎ 01 30 93 00 53
Base nautique de Bonnières, 153 Ile de Gloton Bennecourt

Vernon 27200
Boating
Port d'accueil du Yacht Club, Château des Tourelles:
Base nautique municipale (Mairie), ☎ 01 32 21 16 03
C.N.C.V., 17 quai Camere, ☎ 01 32 51 49 59
Tourist
36 rue Carnot, ☎ 01 32 51 39 60

Notre-Dame-de-l'Isle
Boating
Port Saint Gabriel, Ile Emien, ☎ 01 32 52 64 64

Les Andelys 27700
Boating
Port de plaisance, Quai de Seine, ☎ 01 32 54 21 51
International Marine John Moore, Residence du Grand Parc, BP 318, ☎ 01 32 54 15 29
Ets Boulier, 1 rue Dumont, ☎ 01 32 54 15 52
Garage du Château Gaillard, 22 rue Gil Nicole, ☎ 01 32 54 38 33
Ste Du Val Saint-Martin, 4 rue de Seine, ☎ 01 32 54 40 57
Tourist
24 rue Philippe Auguste, BP 31, ☎ 01 32 54 41 93

Poses
Boating
Base de plein air et de loisirs, ☎ 01 32 59 13 13
Tourist
Remorqueur 'Fauvette' – Association des Anciens et Amis de la Batellerie, ☎ 01 32 59 07 16

St-Aubin-les-Elbeuf 76410
Boating
M. Glancer, 72 rue Scheurer Kestner, 76320 Caudebec-Les-Elbeuf, ☎ 01 35 78 31 70

Rouen 76000
Boating
Ets Bourgeaux, 39 rue St-Sever, ☎ 01 35 72 87 05
Eponville Nautic, Quai d'Elbeuf 76100 Rouen Cedex, ☎ 0135 72 28 24
Demolin, BP 286, 76306 Sotteville-Les-Rouen, ☎ 01 35 72 93 93
Villetard, Ile Lacroix, ☎ 01 35 88 00 00
Tourist
25 place de la Cathédrale, BP 666, ☎ 01 35 71 41 77

Caudebec en Caux 76490
Tourist
Mairie, ave Winston Churchill, BP 83, ☎ 01 35

96 19 84

Honfleur 14600
Boating
Capitainerie du Port, ☎ 01 31 89 20 02
Hue (Ets Gerard) ☎ 01 31 89 38 54, Bassin Ouest quai Carnot
Marine en Bois, Résidence du Levant, ☎ 01 31 89 50 78
Tourist
9 rue de la Ville, ☎ 01 31 89 23 30

Le Havre 76600
Boating
Accostillage Diffusion, 120 rue Augustin Normand, ☎ 01 35 43 43 62
Bisson S.A., 27 quai de Gironde, ☎ 01 35 25 09 21
Chantier Naval de la Baie de Seine, 136 quai Frissard, ☎ 01 35 25 30 51
Cap Marine Plaisance, 105 rue Augustin Normand, ☎ 01 34 42 33 00
Technosea, 7 rue du Docteur Belot, ☎ 01 35 41 30 18
Nautic Service Sauvetage, Z.A.C. de Rogerville, 76700 Harfleur, ☎ 01 35 51 75 30
Mouquet Constructions Metalliques, 82 rue de la Chapelle, 76430 St-Romain de Colbosc, ☎ 01 35 20 02 98/10
Chantier Hauchard Pierre, St-Nicolas de la Taille, 76170 Lillebonne, ☎ 01 35 39 80 37
Roadster Marine, 51 bd de Graville, 76600 Le Havre, ☎ 01 35 26 42 05
Marine Plus, 44 bd Clemenceaux, ☎ 01 35 21 08 06
Tanguy Marine Plus, 31 quai Frissart, ☎ 01 35 25 14 19
Tourist
Place de l'Hôtel de Ville, ☎ 01 35 21 22 88

THE RIVER SEINE
Navigation sub-divisions
Pontoise, 65 quai de L'Ecluse, 95313 St-Ouen-Laumone, ☎ 01 34 64 02 26
Compiègne, 79 barrage de Venette, 60231 Compiègne Cedex, ☎ 01 44 83 21 12

Cergy 95000
Boating
Sonnenschein France S.A., BP 757, ☎ 01 34 64 93 20
Eragny sur Oise 95610
Decarpentrie, 65 chemin de Halage, ☎ 01 34 64 16 65

Pontoise 95300
Boating
Port de Cergy, 6 quai Tourelle, ☎ 01 34 24 11 77
Etablissements Brument, Route de Génicourt, 95650 Boissy L'Aillerie, ☎ 01 34 42 13 86
Roques et Lecoeur Pontoise, 88 rue d'Auvers, ☎ 01 30 38 64 14
Penven, 281 chaussée Jules Cesar, 95250 Beauchamp, ☎ 01 34 13 54 32
Silva France, 12 rue de la Cellophane, 78200 Mantes-La-Ville, ☎ 01 30 92 66 22

Tourist
6 place Petit Martroy, ☎ 01 30 38 24 45

Saint Ouen l'Aumone 95310
Boating
MBM, 74 allée Colbert

L'Isle-Adam-Pamain
Tourist
1 av. de Paris, ☎ 01 34 69 17 06

Beaumont sur Oise 95260
Boating
Croisieres de l'Oise, 5 rue Duquesnel, ☎ 01 30
   34 09 82

Boran sur Oise 60530
Boating
Lefevre, 11 place du Carouge, ☎ 01 44 21 30 00
Nautic Boran (Ets Begaud), 7 place du Carouge,
   ☎ 01 44 21 95 78

St-Leu-d'Esserent 60340
Boating
Base nautique et de plein air, ☎ 01 44 56 61 09
Tourist
rue de l'Eglise, ☎ 01 44 56 38 10

Chantilly 60500
Tourist
av. du Marechal Joffré, ☎ 01 44 57 08 58

Creil 60100
Tourist
Place du General de Gaulle, ☎ 01 44 55 16 07

Nogent sur Oise
Tourist
88 rue General de Gaulle, ☎ 01 44 71 77 70

Villers-St-Paul 60870 Rieux
Boating
Socorel Villers St-Paul, ☎ 01 44 71 58 90

Pont-Ste-Maxence 60700
Tourist
8 rue Fatras, BP 40, ☎ 01 44 72 35 90

Verberie 60410
Boating
Menard, 20 rue de Saintines, ☎ 01 44 40 92 58

Pierrefonds
Tourist
rue Louis d'Orleans, ☎ 01 44 42 81 44

Compiègne 60200
Boating
Guerdin, 13 rue de Clermont, ☎ 01 44 83 35 57
Tourist
6 place de l'Hôtel de Ville, ☎ 01 44 40 01 00
Sarl Le Compiègne, 23 rue du Chant des
   Cosaques, ☎ 01 49 77 62 19
Janville 60150 Thourotte
Boating
Chantiers Pruvost, Ile Jean-Lenoble Janville, ☎
   01 44 76 01 71

Index